Jack

www.myspace.com/jackcotaling

15, Davisburg, MI

Just think. Think about everything that you do and what impact it has on the environment. Then think about what you can do to change that. It's really simple.

myspace

OurPlanet

CHANGE IS POSSIBLE

BY THE

MYSPACE COMMUNITY
WITH JECA TAUDTE

FOREWORD BY

TOM ANDERSON

The Bowen Press   Collins   HARPER TEEN

An Imprint of HarperCollins Publishers

MySpace Project Managers: Liba Rubenstein and Lindsay Tredent

MySpace Editor: Micah Fitzerman-Blue

HarperTeen and Collins are imprints of HarperCollins Publishers.

MySpace/OurPlanet
Text and art copyright © 2008 by HarperCollins Publishers

The editors have made every effort to include the user names of everyone who contributed an "eco-tip" on the MySpace/Our Planet page. The contributors' names appear beginning on p. 162. Any eco-tips published in this book were used with permission and are reprinted verbatim.

Library of Congress Cataloging-in-Publication Data is available.

ISBN 978-0-06-156204-4

Art by Dan Santat
Design by Edward Miller
❖
First Edition

HarperCollins is actively working to reduce its impact on climate change. We are transforming the way we use energy and working with our partners to take action. We're still very much at the beginning of our work, but we have full confidence that, in time, we will be able to reshape ourselves as a greener—and more efficient—publishing company.

MySpace/Our Planet: Change Is Possible is part of News Corporation's Global Energy Initiative to reduce the company's impact on the climate and engage its audiences on the issue. For more information on News Corporation's Global Energy Initiative or to learn more about what MySpace and HarperCollins are doing to reduce their own impact on climate change, visit www.newscorp.com/energy.

For all the friends of our planet

Contents

myspace

OurPlanet

Foreword

Hi Guys,

Tom here. :) You might be as surprised as I am that I'm writing in a book instead of a blog. But I wouldn't be doing this unless I thought it was for something so unbelievably important that it had to be in print.

It's pretty clear that unless we do something, and fast, we could be damaging the Earth beyond the point where it could repair itself. I don't need to tell you that this is a huge problem, maybe the most important issue of our generation.

But we can do something. This book is a guide to the small steps that we can take every single day to save our environment from damage and destruction. You may not realize how many choices you make each day that directly affect the planet. Everything from the clothes you buy to the food you eat, to the way you spend your birthday has an impact. Even your lint has an impact. (Don't believe me? Turn to p. 35.)

The MySpace community certainly makes a difference. At 200 million strong and growing, we have a unique opportunity to change things for the better (you non-MySpace users are always welcome to join us). We hit the books, consulted the pros, drank a lot of coffee, and crammed these pages with the most useful and interesting info we could find. The idea is to turn you into an expert.

One more thing: this book is not just an eco-guide. It's also a really long thank-you note to one of MySpace's most active and vital communities, OurPlanet. Hand-in-hand with MySpace Impact, OurPlanet is the place where users work together with environmental organizations to transform interest into action. Without their energy and enthusiasm, none of this would be possible. You can see their input on every page. They've changed the way we do things here at MySpace, and we're really grateful.

They also helped us with the title.

Your Friend,

Tom Anderson
MySpace.com/Tom

1. Our Planet

1 Degree So Far

The science is clear: It's getting hot in here—but keep your clothes on, and pay attention. This is serious. The average global temperature has increased by 1 degree Fahrenheit over the last century. Even worse, scientists predict that the global average temperature will continue to rise between 2 and 11.5 degrees Fahrenheit by 2100.

One degree? 11.5 degrees? That may not sound like a lot, but the Earth's temperature has not changed so dramatically since the last ice age 20,000 years ago. We're already feeling the impact all over the world. On every continent, hotter average temperatures are melting ice sheets, expanding deserts, and changing weather patterns. The major cause of all this change is greenhouse gas emissions—particularly carbon dioxide (aka CO_2), the most common and dangerous greenhouse gas.

What's behind these CO_2 emissions? We are. If there is one thing we're all good at, it's making carbon dioxide. Whenever we burn fossil fuels, we release CO_2 into the atmosphere. Right now, the level of CO_2 in the atmosphere is at a level that has not been equaled in the last 650,000 years. Way to go, humanity.

Global warming is here—and it's going to get worse unless something is done to stop it. (This is where you come in.)

Face the Facts

Less than 20 years ago the idea that our planet was warming because of human activity seemed absurd to many people. Less than 20 years ago, people also liked parachute pants, so let's cut them *some* slack. Today, as the scientific case for global climate change grows, the facts don't lie:

- Since 1979 more than one-fifth of the polar ice cap has melted.
- Eleven of the twelve warmest years on record were from 1995 to 2006.
- The number of large wildfires in the western United States has quadrupled in the last 35 years as the average "fire season" has grown two months longer. The California wildfires of 2007 were some of the fiercest on record.

It gets worse. More alarming than the fact that global warming is happening is what will happen next. If nothing is done, scientists predict that:

- There will be no glaciers left in Montana's Glacier National Park by 2030.
- The global sea level will be at least 3 feet higher by the end of the century.
- Roughly a quarter of plant and animal species will be at risk of extinction if temperatures rise more than 4.5 degrees Fahrenheit.

3 Worst-Case Scenarios

Of course, there's no certainty about when or even if the events below might occur, but they are considered to be "tipping points"— irreversible scenarios after which human effort may be unable to stop climate change:

Worst-case scenario No. 1: A widespread coral bleaching from rising sea temperatures that would damage our planet's fisheries. *Potential time frame: 30 years.*

Worst-case scenario No. 2: A rise in sea level of 20 feet from the melting of the Greenland or West Antarctic ice sheets. This would leave coastal regions all over the world flooded as if by a permanent tsunami.
Potential time frame: next two centuries.

Worst-case scenario No. 3: A shutdown of the Atlantic Ocean's thermohaline current, which keeps Europe's temperatures moderate and determines the Atlantic's water temperatures.
Potential time frame: 200 years.

The Skinny: Carbon Dioxide

Carbon dioxide is a naturally occurring gas. You just exhaled some (but don't hold your breath—we need you around). Trees, plants, and oceans drink it in, serving as carbon "sinks" for the CO_2 that's in our atmosphere. They also release it, or its molecular parts, in what's known as the natural carbon cycle. Whatever CO_2 is in our atmosphere traps the sun's energy as part of the greenhouse gas effect, heating our planet. For all of human history this has been good. Naturally occurring greenhouse gases have kept our planet warm enough for human life.

It's the *unnaturally* occurring greenhouse gases that pose a problem. For starters, there's way too much of it. Current CO_2 levels are 30 times greater than they were before the Industrial Revolution ushered in the widespread use of burning fossil fuels. (For more on the Industrial Revolution, ask a really old person.) These high levels of CO_2 are trapping more energy, causing global warming. Pound for pound, we are carbon gluttons.

My Annual Weight-Loss Program (measured in CO_2 emissions)
- Use one 60-watt incandescent bulb at home: 180 lbs.
- Use one gallon of gas: 20 lbs.
- Shower for eight minutes a day for a year: 1,368 lbs.
- Run your air conditioner at 72 degrees Fahrenheit in the summer: 2,263 lbs.
- Dry your laundry in an electric dryer (annual average): 1,446 lbs.
- Fly from New York to Los Angeles: 2,000 lbs.
- Drive 10,000 miles in a Chevy Malibu: 17,000 lbs.
- Live in America (annual average): 22,000 lbs.

What You Can Do

Climate change is a global problem. But we all have a part to play. Nearly everything we do—driving, watching TV, cooking dinner, dancing naked in the street—has an impact on the environment. (Well, maybe not the last one.) The sum of the CO_2 emissions that stem from our actions is our carbon footprint—the amount of carbon we're individually responsible for. By reducing your carbon footprint, you can play a critical role in stopping global warming.

The most basic way for you to reduce your carbon footprint is to decrease the amount of energy you use. Doing that starts with small simple changes in your habits—like the way you get to school or the way you shower. Where it ends is up to you.

But don't be fooled. The level of action any individual can make is micro compared to the macro efforts—by governments, by industries, and by entire countries of people—that need to be made. Your efforts alone will never be enough. That's because environmental revolution is what's called for—system-wide. If global warming is really going to be stopped, our government on local, national, and global levels must get involved. Our corporations must do their part, our farmers theirs. But you're more important than you think you are.

Because without your micro efforts—and those of everyone around you—those sweeping system-wide changes are unlikely to happen. So the point is not that everyone do everything. It's that everyone do something.

It's your choice. Your actions can contribute to the climate crisis facing our planet—or they can play a meaningful part in stopping it. But if you're going to live, shop, party, travel, and learn in more eco-friendly ways, it's time to get started.

The Big Question: Why is it our problem? Haven't we got this under control?

Myth: Developed countries like the United States are not going to be the biggest global warming offenders in the near future.

Truth: It's true that developing countries—especially India and China—have the fastest rising emissions rates. The annual emissions of developing countries are projected to eclipse the emissions of developed countries, such as the United States or Japan, in the next 10 years. But China's per person emissions are projected to be only a quarter of U.S. rates in 2025. That means that each person in America is expected to be *four times* as carbon-crazy as each person in China. And it adds up: Total U.S. emissions are estimated to be 28 percent higher in 2025 than they are today.

*((**!!This is just the begining!!**))*
www.myspace.com/jesicajensen
14, Illinois

picture the world as a huge bed, would you want to sleep in a bed that has been poluted with garbage and dangeruse chemicals? we only have one world, when we kill this one we cant get another!!!

Coty
www.myspace.com/xx_coty_xx
19, Bowling Green, KY

The bottom line to all this is that most people in this world are too lazy to care enough to change certain things they do already to better others in the world in which they live. Sure they might think about their future children and grand children but apparently not enough. A saying that I hear a lot is the fact that they won't be around that long to see the change so why should they care.

I wish there was an easier way to get everyone to start caring.

Erika [♥]
www.myspace.com/blanc_lapin
19, Norwich, CT

Practice and promote stewardship. Stewardship is the act of taking care of something that isn't yours (such as out planet); to meet the needs of the present generation, without compromising the needs of future generations.

Angela
www.myspace.com/opreflector
41

What are we without our precious planet? Where would we go if we lost that? It only makes common sense to take care of our ONLY home

MySpace Action

Your MySpace page can be a window into your eco-friendly soul—
that and your blog about how funny your cat is. Here are just a few
ways you can make your MySpace profile "green" (besides making
everything the color green):

- Use pics and wallpaper that make it clear that the Earth matters to
  you.
- List environmental activists among your heroes.
- Pick songs to play on your MySpace profile by musicians who are
  vocal about the environment.
- Ditto for listing books and movies by eco-friendly celebs.
- Make sure that at least one environmental organization (or
  MySpace's OurPlanet page) is in your Top Eight.

2. Health and Body
It's More Than Skin Deep

How are you feeling? A little warm? You're not alone. Our health is linked to the health of the environment. The costs of climate change don't register just in inches of acid rain or Arctic ice density. High rates of cancer and diabetes suggest that our modern lifestyle has an effect on our bodies as well as our forests, oceans, and air. But with some planning, we can treat ourselves and our planet better than we do today.

Face the Facts

Beauty is big business, dahling: Americans spend more than $2.6 billion on hair products and $8 billion on cosmetics each year (and yet, we still can't find a date). That's a lot of makeup, and there's nothing compact about the amount of waste this produces. Just consider the boxes your toothpaste tube comes in. Why do they have to put a *tube* in a *box*?! In fact:

- Two billion disposable razors are purchased annually. And because they're disposable they'll eventually make their way to the landfill.
- An estimated 50 million lbs. of toothbrushes are deposited in landfills every year—not to mention the miles and miles of floss.

What You Can Do

It's possible to look, smell, and feel good while allowing our planet to do the same.

Don't be lazy. Take the stairs rather than the elevator. Walk or bike rather than drive. It's more eco-friendly and it's better for your body. (But you should still do something about your hair.) *micro*

Stop hitting the bottle. *Water* bottle, obviously. Bottled water isn't guaranteed to be any better for you than tap water. (For more on why, see pp. 21–22.) Plus, all those plastic bottles are piling up—75 percent of them in landfills. In comparison, consider how much less waste is generated when you turn on the faucet. *micro*

Refill 'er up. Invest in a reusable water bottle or an aluminum mug or Thermos for tea and coffee. You'll drink less bottled water and you'll reduce the environmental impact from all those paper cups your hot drinks come in. *micro*

Dispose of the disposable habits. Go with shavers that have disposable blades or even try electric models. (Just be sure to unplug your bathroom electronics when you're not using them.) Also, look for toothbrushes made from recycled plastic. *micro*

Read the label. Look at any bottle of shampoo or stick of deodorant. How many words on the ingredients list can you pronounce? Odds are, if you can't pronounce them, they may not be the most eco-friendly. (For more on which ingredients you should always avoid, see p. 19.) You'll be on your way to better health faster than you can say hydroquinone. *micro*

Ditch the fossil-fuel face and skin. Petroleum jelly and mineral oil are rather pretty ways of referring to the thick black liquid gold each of those products are made from. Avoid skin products made from petroleum. You wouldn't go to the local gas station and douse yourself in gas, so why would you slather it on in your bathroom? *micro*

Skip the gym. Sure you've noticed that the treadmill or stationary bike you use at the gym is plugged into the wall. But did you realize that all the electricity you're using to exercise could be saved if you ran or biked or climbed stairs outside the gym? Also, you wouldn't look like a hamster. *micro*

Eat organic. Eat local, fresh, and organic. By eating local and organic foods, you can often reduce the emissions associated with transporting foods from the other side of the globe as well as the chemicals involved in producing the food in the first place. Getting your family to set an organic table may be hard, however, since organic food can be pricey. But the savings that come from buying less and cooking at home should more than make up for these costs. Plus, when your parents see you eating local vegetables rather than preserved potato chips, they may just go for it themselves. *MACRO*

(freaak_nasty) A. DOANut
www.myspace.com/freaak_nasty
17, Carlsbad, CA

Well what my family does, is we shower every other day. It may seem nasty, but trust me most of us don't need to shower twice a day. Also when your waiting for you shower to get warm, you can place a bucket underneath to catch all the cold water your wasting and use it to water your plants. Just think of all the good water you'll be able to conserve!!!

!ash!
www.myspace.com/perfectxcold
15, Nashville, IN

I tie a green string around my bracelet, then it reminds me to hurry up ,in the shower, turn off the lights, ect. It's a great way to remember about global warming!

Kristi
www.myspace.com/kldkdoc
36, Mesa, AZ

I envision a place where I could have my shampoo, conditioner, lotions etc. refilled, like a filling station, rather than buying a new PLASTIC bottle every time!

Go beyond the basics to treat yourself and our planet in more eco-friendly ways.

Your Edible Environment

Our planet's land, oceans, and animals provide us with everything we eat. (Except for Cheez Whiz, which is made by aliens.) Eco-friendly eating is possible if you ask all of your food one simple question: How did you get here? Consider what was required to get that food into your local store or on the menu, and choose the less fertilized, less traveled, and less refrigerated option.

Get fresh. Frozen food uses 10 times more energy to produce than fresh food. Plus it's more likely to taste like freezer burn than the fresh fruit or vegetable it once was.

Keep it close to home. Supermarkets dupe you into thinking that all food should be available at all times, regardless of the season. For them, it's nothing to ship your strawberries halfway around the world in January. But it's a problem for our planet. Buying food that's grown, harvested, and prepared locally means it has probably traveled less, has required less energy to preserve it, and may have less packaging. If possible, shop for produce at your local farmers market.

Super(eco)market shopping. Look for eco-friendly options at the supermarket. Try to buy food with less packaging. Is the loaf of bread double-bagged? Is the box that pasta comes in recyclable? Choose a glass, steel, or aluminum jar or can instead of a plastic jug or bottle. Now invite us over. We like pie.

Make your steak rare. Eating less meat is one way to follow an eco-friendly diet. Significant amounts of water, grain, land, and labor are required to get meat on the table. One pound of beef uses 12,000 gallons of water. Compare this to 60 gallons for a pound of potatoes. Cut down slowly and look into high-protein alternatives like beans and tofu. Hey, don't knock it till you try it.

Fish (not phish) around. The fishing industry has plundered our oceans like a gold-greedy pirate. Today many fish populations are in danger and knowing which fish to keep off your plate may help them survive. Visit www.mbayaq.org/cr/seafoodwatch.asp for more information.

Most Eco-Friendly Organic Fruits & Veggies

Peaches	Celery	Lettuces
Apples	Nectarines	Pears
Sweet bell peppers	Strawberries	Spinach
	Cherries	Potatoes

little pink boo[x]RELOADED[x]
www.myspace.com/eva_chan
19, King Boo's Manor, Cocoa (Keeling) Islands

simply being a vegetarian or vegan makes a great difference. so much land and resources are used up just to feed one omnivore and by not consuming meat, one chooses not to support big industries

alicia

www.myspace.com/butterfliesandhurricanes218, =|,

Kentucky

In order to lead a more eco-friendly life I participate in a vegan lifestyle! The processing of animal products is overwhelming detrimental to the environment and I don't support them in any way. Going veg is good for the earth!=)

Good News/Bad News: Local Food Movement

Locavores, or 100-mile dieters, are people who restrict their diet to food that originates close to home—that is, no more than 100 miles away. They believe that one way to be a more eco-friendly eater is to adopt a rigid approach to the local food movement. When held up against the pesticide and fertilizer-dripping heft of big agribusiness, their arguments sound solid. But a rigid approach may not be as peachy as it sounds at first.

The argument: Eat local food, produced by local farms. Your food tastes better and is healthier for you. Also, you'll curb CO_2 emissions because the food doesn't have to be shipped so far.

Where it gets fuzzy: What's green—and what's greener? Organic food crated and shipped from South America or local food that's been treated with pesticide and then shipped to your market from a farm down the road? Is one good for you, while the other's good for the planet?

Consider: The best of both worlds, local *and* organic, may be an option. If not, then make a decision based on what your priorities are—don't sweat your choice. The fact that you're even thinking about which option's better means you're way ahead of the shmoes who don't think about any of this stuff.

Your Temple of Toiletries . . . er, the Bathroom

It's a toss-up to decide which has more complicated—and possibly more toxic—ingredients: the bottle in your bathroom cabinet, or the harsh cleansers under your kitchen sink. Sure, the bathroom shelf may *smell* nicer, but a rose isn't always a rose.

As you make your personal care more eco-friendly, start with the basic principle: Be simple. That means go for fewer ingredients, shorter ingredient names, and even fewer products.

To see what's in your shampoo, shaving gel, toothpaste, or lotion, go to Skin Deep, a searchable, online database of personal care products maintained by the Environmental Working Group: www.cosmeticsdatabase.com or www.myspace.com/ourplanet.

Ingredients to Avoid:

- **Coal-tar colors**—coal-tar chemicals are often listed as "FD&C" or "D&C" colors. Found in some makeup and hair dye.
- **Formaldehyde**—found in eye shadows, mascaras, and other cosmetics
- **Mercury**—a possible carcinogen that's often listed as "thimerosal." Found in some eyedrops, ointments, and mascaras.
- **Placenta**—contain hormones that can interfere with the body's natural hormone levels. Found in some hair relaxers, moisturizers, and toners.
- **Lead acetate**—a known toxin that's banned in the European Union. Found in some hair dyes and cleansers.
- **Petrochemicals**—aka petrolatum, mineral oil, and paraffin. May contain known or possible carcinogens. Found in some hair relaxers, shampoos, anti-aging creams, mascaras, perfumes, foundations, lipsticks, and lip balms.
- **Phthalates**—these chemicals make plastic softer and more flexible. They may also change the hormonal balance and activity of humans. Found in some nail polishes, fragrances, and hair sprays. Other phthalates to watch for include dimethyl phthalate (DMP) and diethyl phthalate (DEP). To avoid them, try "fragrance-free" options.
- **Hydroquinone**—a possible carcinogen that affects the skin. Found in some skin-lightening products and moisturizers.
- **Nanoparticles**—super-tiny particles that can be absorbed into the bloodstream because they're so small. Found in some sunscreens, bronzers, eye shadows, and lotions.

Sweat the Small Stuff

Living a more eco-friendly lifestyle can help you stay in shape if you're biking, walking, and eating more organic fruits and vegetables. As you tone those washboard abs of yours, try these out:

Hydrate with tap water. You don't need froufy designer water to replenish what you sweat out. Take a reusable water bottle with you as you pound the pavement or get a water-container attachment for your bike. (Why? See pp. 21–22.)

Time your workout to limit showering. Showering more than once a day wastes a lot of water—a 10-minute shower can use more than 25 gallons of water—plus the energy needed to heat all those gallons.

Celebrate "Bring Your Towel to Workout Day." If you use a gym, bring your own towel and skip the in-house towel service. Like hotels, gyms wash and dry towels after one use—using water and energy and releasing harsh chemicals from the detergents into the environment.

Keep it clean—but not too clean. Do you really need to wash your jeans every time you wear them? Do our planet a favor and wash your clothes when they're dirty—not before.

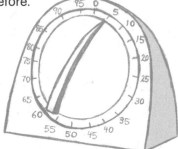

The Big Question:
Tap the faucet or the bottle?

We're told to drink eight glasses of water each day and we must be listening. More than 70 million bottles of water are consumed each day in the United States. But while drinking water is healthy—healthier than downing sodas and maybe even juice and milk—all that plastic ain't so healthy for our planet.

So what should you do—buy your water or sip from the spigot?

Myth: Bottled water is purer and healthier than the water you get out of your tap.

Truth: While it's true that some U.S. water systems are not as clean as others, it's not true that bottled water is always going to be cleaner. Bottled water comes in several types—mineral, spring, sparkling, artesian, purified, and well water. Some bottled water is simply filtered tap water. The water in Aquafina bottles, for example, comes from the municipal water systems of Detroit and Fresno, among other cities. Yum. Educate yourself about what's in the bottle and what comes out of the spigot before you take the next sip.

To find out more about your local tap water, go to www.epa.gov/safewater/dwinfo/index.

Myth: If bottled water is good for your health, it must be good for our planet.

Truth: In 2006, Americans spent nearly $11 billion on more than 8 billion gallons of bottled water. Then we tossed three out of four of those plastic bottles in the trash. Not only do those bottles fill up precious landfill space, but their manufacture drains 1.5 million barrels of oil each year. Not yet convinced it's a bad idea? Swallow this: It takes two liters of water to make one liter of bottled water. That means for every bottle of water you drink, twice the amount has been consumed in the manufacturing process.

Dawn
www.myspace.com/palmtreesrain
14, Southern Jongmu Temple, Colorado

My main contribution to protect our enviroment this year is giving up bottle water completely. This was huge change for me. I normally drink about a case of bottled water a month. I now carry a water container and fill it with filter water from my home. It is strange how I now look at those who have a bottle of water in their hand and wonder if they know how bad that bottle of water impacts our planet.

Going Green (a real-life story)

The Teens for Safe Cosmetics (www.teens4sc.org) campaign wants to give the makeup industry a makeover. This teen-led initiative based in Marin County, California, is part of the larger cancer awareness group Search for the Cause. In 2005, Jessica Assaf and a group of friends organized Operation Beauty Drop, which placed bins in public spaces for other teens to toss their cosmetics into. The bins were then shipped back to their manufacturers with petitions demanding safer products. They also lobbied California's governor on behalf of SB484, the Safe Cosmetics Act of 2005. Thanks to their efforts, California became the first state in the nation to pass a safe cosmetics law. The group has also held an educational summit and continues to educate the public throughout the Bay Area on the possible dangers of many cosmetic products.

Do This Right Now

[green] Go a week without buying bottled water by carrying a reusable container. Then go another week.

[greener] Adopt a dryer-less hairstyle.

[greenest] Research what's in your shampoo, lotion, and toothpaste. Depending on your results, consider if there's a less-toxic option and go with that.

Miss Andi
www.myspace.com/wildeyedpixie
17, Kansas City, MO

My family buys organic food from a local farmer - no pesticides and very little transportation pollution. Plus, we're eating food that's in season!

if only you knew. <!>
www.myspace.com/akjg
21, Arizona

Knowing my food didn't say "ow" before it ended up on my plate makes it much more edible.

MySpace Action

Keep a MySpace blog about your week of eco-eating. Take pics of your dishes and post recipes for others. Do your best to consume local and/or organic foods and avoid items with excess throwaway packaging. Wanna go the whole nine yards? Make a cooking show and post it on MySpaceTV.

3. Your Home, Your Planet

Your Home. Your Planet. (Your Home Planet?)

Next to your body, your home is the place you have the most control over—and where your efforts to be more eco-friendly can have the most immediate impact. Don't believe us? Check out the groove in the couch that perfectly conforms to your butt. Now *that's* control.

Think about it: You can't easily get the mall to change its thermostat and waste less energy (if you can even find the mall's thermostat)—at least not without getting arrested. But you can make changes in your room, your yard, and your kitchen. In fact, you can take simple steps and make nearly every nook and cranny in your house more eco-friendly.

Face the Facts

Your home is likely where you use the most energy and water and where you create the most waste.

- We're #1. Americans spend more than $160 billion—45 percent of our energy costs—a year to heat, cool, light, and operate all the gadgets in our homes. Together, our heating and cooling systems emit 150 million tons of carbon dioxide into the atmosphere each year.

- The average American uses 100 gallons of water a day for cleaning, cooking, and drinking.

- We're pretty trashy. The average American generates 4.5 lbs. of trash every day.

All of this adds up. America has been responsible for nearly a quarter of the globe's total CO_2 emissions for years. On average, each American is responsible for 22,000 lbs.—that's 11 tons—of CO_2 emissions per year.

What You Can Do

Junk the junk mail. Who needs it? Unless you collect car-insurance offers and pre-approved credit cards, get your family's names off of junk-mail lists. Go to www.dmaconsumers.org (catalogs and magazines), www.optoutprescreen.com (credit bureaus), and www.directmail.com/directory/mail_preference/ (National Do Not Mail List). To stop getting catalogs you don't want, email optout@abacus-direct.com. (micro)

Go cold. Ninety percent of the energy you use washing clothes goes to heating the water. Wash your clothes in cold water and save your family up to $63 a year in bills. (micro)

Get turned on. The average home has about 30 light fixtures. That means 30 or more lightbulbs sucking electricity. If you replace three frequently used conventional lightbulbs with compact fluorescent lightbulbs (CFL), you could save 300 lbs. of CO_2 and $60 per year. Replace all of them and save 10 times more money and carbon dioxide emissions. It's win-win. (micro)

Pull the plug. Plugged-in appliances use energy even when they're not on. Simply unplugging small appliances like your cell phone, iPod, Xbox 360, life-sized Gumby robot, and electric can opener can save more than 1,000 lbs. of carbon dioxide and $256 per year. Besides, who uses an electric can opener anyways? (Answer: Robot Gumby) *micro*

Shut the fridgin' door. Refrigerators across America consume the same amount of electricity that's generated by 25 large power plants every year. Opening the fridge door allows up to 30 percent of the chilled air inside to escape, forcing the refrigerator to hum harder. So before opening the door, consider what you want and where it is. Also, make sure the internal thermostats are set to energy-saving settings and keep the coils at the back clean to increase efficiency. *micro*

Shorten your shower. We've been through this, but we think you need to hear it again. Hot showers are responsible for two-thirds of your water heating costs. If you shorten your shower, you could save 350 lbs. of CO_2 emissions and $99 per year. *micro*

Choose greener energy. Some energy providers offer energy created from renewable sources, not just fossil fuels. Check with your local provider to see what's on their alternative energy menu. For more information, go to www.epa.gov/greenpower/locator or www.green-e.org. *MACRO*

shannon (sox over rox)
www.myspace.com/187677501
16, the ville,Uzbekistan

For all the ladies (and guys if you're into that), try not running the water in the shower while shaving your legs. Saving a little water one hair at a time.

*[A|A{N}G[Y] ^_____^*
www.myspace.com/airbender503

Limit the amount of toilet paper you use. You really don't need twenty sheets to wipe your bum.

We've covered the basics, now let's get down to the nitty-gritty.

Your Room

Nice digs. Of course we know you just threw all your junk in your closet before we came in. But it's not the decorating we're concerned about. Take a critical look around: What does your room say about you and the environment? Your room doesn't have to be filled with organic, natural, or recycled things to be green (although it's great if it is). Here are two simple steps you can take to show your concern for and commitment to preventing climate change.

Go on a power strip. Make sure you plug your stereo, computer, TV, and game consoles into a power strip so you can conveniently turn all your electronics off before you go to sleep or head out for the day.

Go blinds. Put the blinds down or close the curtains to keep the sun out in the summer. This will reduce your cooling costs. Do the same thing in the winter when there's no sun to help insulate your room from drafts. If you get direct sun, let it shine and that will help heat the room.

Serena Matthews
www.myspace.com/serenamatthews
Nashville, TN

It's simple. If I'm not using a light, I turn it off. How much easier can it get than that?

[hey] it's aj™
www.myspace.com/aj_is_the_bomb_digity
14, Owasso, OK

when you leave the house, turn off your tvs and lights and radios. your dog doesnt need them :)

The Bathroom

We've already touched on products you use in the loo. Now let's talk about the place itself and what you can do to further green your grooming:

Waste less water. Cut the concert off, Sinatra, and take shorter showers. Consider turning off the water while soaping up or shampooing. Don't run the water while you're brushing your teeth (unless you're about to shave, in which case you can brush your teeth while the water's heating up). If you take a bath, only fill the tub halfway.

Or just skip out. Americans take more showers (and have drier skin) than anyone else on Earth. Skip the shower once in a while. Our planet (and your skin) will thank you.

If it's yellow . . . Every time you flush the toilet, you use from 2 to 5 gallons of water. If everyone in America flushed one time less each day, we could save more than 500 million gallons of water. But if flushing less often isn't an option, consider making each flush use less water with low-flush mechanisms. You can buy one of these or simply fill a small bottle with sand and put it in your tank.

Unplug the (electricity) drain. A bathroom appliance isn't much different from any other appliance (except, hopefully, it's waterproof). Electric toothbrushes, electric shavers, and hair dryers can all use phantom electricity and should be unplugged when not in use or charging.

The Kitchen

The triple threat of energy, water, and waste come together in a big way in the kitchen. To minimize the impact on the environment:

Compost your cares away. We throw away 96 billion lbs. of food a year. That's more than a quarter of the food we produce. Even though most of it is wasted outside individual homes, composting at home is a small step toward turning food waste into something productive like fertilizer. Choose to compost rather than run the disposal, which wastes water. To learn more about composting, check out www.howtocompost.org.

Bus better. Run your dishwasher only when it's full. Choose the air-dry option rather than the heated dry cycle. And shorten your clean-up time: Don't pre-wash or rinse your dishes before you put them in the dishwasher. After all, that's what the dog's for.

The Skinny: Recycling

Lose virginity: recycle. In 2005, America's recycling efforts saved 79 million tons of waste material from going into landfills and incinerators. But not only does recycling mean reduced space in landfills, reincarnation takes less energy and water than manufacturing virgin (from scratch) products. Consider:

- Recycling a stack of newspapers 3 feet high saves one tree.
- Recycling aluminum cans saves 95 percent of the energy required to produce a virgin can.
- Recycling one glass container saves enough energy to power a conventional lightbulb for 4 hours—or a CFL bulb for 20 hours. And a ton of recycled glass saves the equivalent of nine gallons of fuel oil.
- Recycling five plastic soda bottles provides enough fiber to make an extra large T-shirt or 1 square foot of carpet.

Change is possible: Twenty years ago, only one curbside recycling program existed in the United States. In 2005 nearly 9,000 curbside programs had been established across the country.

To learn more about your local recycling options go to www.nrc-recycle.org.

Your Yard

Many of the changes you can make to help the environment mean doing less. But in your backyard, think about doing more: more trees, more plants, more physical activity.

Plant trees. Trees use what we need less of: carbon dioxide. The more trees in your yard, the more CO_2 taken out of the atmosphere. Planting them is one way to begin offsetting your carbon emissions locally and on your own: Each tree will use 2,000 lbs. of CO_2 a year and an estimated ton of CO_2 over its lifetime.

This ain't no putting green. Rather than pouring on water and fertilizers in pursuit of a pristine lawn, go more natural with native bushes and trees. When the planting is well planned, thicker vegetation can cut heating and cooling costs by providing shade and reducing wind. Besides, reducing the size of your lawn means cutting down on cutting the grass.

Push it. Use a push mower to cut what grass you do have. It uses less gas, emits 80 lbs. less CO_2 per year than a rider mower, and gives your legs some much-needed exercise. We do it. Have you *seen* our calves lately?

Out of the Closet

Closets can hold anything—clothes, shoes, stereos, comics, and dead bodies. That's what makes them great. It's also what makes them dead-ends (get it?) for our best eco-intentions. Here's a list of things you can do to prevent having a closet full of eco-skeletons (get it?!):

De-lint. U.S. households can already spend up to $135 a year on energy drying clothes. A dirty lint filter can cause the dryer to use 30 percent more energy than a clean one. Also, don't overload the dryer. It will have to work harder and less efficiently. Or really do our planet a favor and hang your clothes out to dry. (They'll smell better, too.)

Be neighborly. You may not want all the crap in your closet, but you'd be surprised how many of your neighbors might. Communities are setting up online mechanisms to connect with their neighbors. Check out www.freecycle.com and www.myspace.com/planetaid.

Don't dry-clean. Dry cleaners often use a harmful chemical called perc (perchloroethylene), so if you do dry-clean, try to air out your clothes before you hang them up. Also, ask for no plastic bags when you pick up your clothes. Return your hangers to your dry cleaner for recycling.

Kyle O-Saurus
www.myspace.com/ksmothedino
19, Orlando, FL

Only dry shirts and jeans in a dryer for about 10 minutes, then hang them to dry. This conserves energy used while washing and drying your clothes.

The Big Question: Green energy or fossil fuels?

Electricity generation is the leading cause of industrial air pollution in the United States. That's because the majority of our electricity comes from coal, nuclear, and other fossil fuel power plants. Renewable electricity comes from sources that are infinite like the sun, wind, tides, or other sources that replenish themselves naturally. They are also often clean or green because, unlike fossil fuels, they don't emit CO_2 and other pollutants.

The five main types of renewable energy sources are solar, wind, hydroelectric, biomass, and geothermal. Of these, solar, wind, and hydro are cleanest.

Myth: Changing to green energy involves getting a new energy company that's smaller and less reliable.

Truth: Many, although not all, energy companies now offer green options. To switch to cleaner energy, you can simply sign up for the one that best meets your family's needs.

If your local energy company does not offer options to buy green energy directly, consider buying renewable energy credits (RECs) or green tags. Green tags help clean power generators offset the higher cost of producing clean energy—which brings us to the next myth of renewable energy: the cost.

Myth: Green energy is way too expensive to be a viable alternative.

Truth: Renewable energy does cost more to produce than energy that comes from fossil fuel. But it's not prohibitively more expensive. In New York City an average residential customer using 350 kilowatt-hours of electricity per month would pay $3.50 more each month for a mix of wind and hydro power than standard electricity. That's only, like, 3½ Neil Diamond songs on iTunes.

Myth: If my family buys green power, we will be more eco-friendly than our neighbors.

Truth: Because of the way energy delivery works, buying green or clean electricity from your local energy company means that your regional grid, not your house, will have cleaner energy. Why do it then? Buying green energy helps fund the development of sustainable energy delivery systems. And that means that you and your neighbors and your entire community can cut your CO_2 emissions. You're not keeping up with the Joneses, you're forcing them to keep up with you.

Do This Right Now

[green] Raise your lighting average. There are probably 30 light fixtures in your house. If you've installed CFLs in three of them, then you're 10 percent of the way toward total eco-friendly lighting. Double your effort with three more and you'll move up to 20 percent. You'll also reduce your yearly CO_2 emissions by about 3 percent on average.

[greener] Shave three minutes off your shower. Spending less time in the shower will save both water and the energy needed to heat the water. In fact, showering for five minutes or less saves up to 1,000 gallons a month. How close can you get to a five-minute shower?

[greenest] Put your trash can on a diet. The average American family generates more than 100 lbs. of trash a week. Bring your bathroom scale outside. See if you can cut down on the amount of garbage you create in one week by weighing your trash bag. Then see if you can keep those pounds off for a month.

Free Space
www.myspace.com/coloradosurf
26, Colorado

For one week, carry all the trash that you generate yourself. this will show how much is truley wasted, and once you see how much waste you produce, you just might start looking at redundant packaging closer.

Good News/Bad News: Going Carbon Neutral

Reducing your carbon footprint completely through your personal efforts probably isn't possible in our current society. (We suppose you could always live in a cave.) Does the new trend of carbon offsetting offer a way to balance out what you can't reduce? Well, *maybe*.

How it works: First tally up your own carbon footprint. There are a number of footprint calculators online. (See p. 152 for a list.) Then offset by paying for a product that, in theory, stores the same amount of CO_2 and makes you "carbon neutral."

You can offset your carbon in any number of ways: choosing renewable energy projects with wind or solar power, supporting energy-efficiency programs, or investing in reforestation projects. Carbon offsetting works because it pools resources of people who want to do something, but who aren't able to build a windmill, for instance, on their own.

How it doesn't work: Going carbon neutral might feel great, but offsetting is not a get-out-of-hot-planet-prison-free card. It should never be the first step on the eco-friendly path. Think of it more like the last thing you do after you've done everything you can to shrink your carbon footprint.

What's the problem with trees? It's true that trees absorb CO_2, and large forests act as "carbon sinks," washing CO_2 from the atmosphere and replacing it with oxygen. But offsetting strategies that call for widespread tree planting are controversial—and possibly ineffective. Studies suggest that successful reforesting efforts may vary by geographic region. Plus the lag time between the carbon emissions you cause and the time when their equivalent are absorbed in a tree planted now may not provide real balance.

When Coldplay (www.myspace.com/coldplay) produced their second album, *A Rush of Blood to the Head*, they elected to total up and neutralize the CO_2 they emitted while making the album. They paid for 10,000 mango trees to be planted in Karnataka, India. But their good efforts didn't bear fruit: 40 percent of the saplings died because of a lack of water. If the trees had lived, it would have been decades before they reached their full carbon offsetting potential.

Offset with reputable companies. A green gold rush has led offsetting companies to sprout up by the dozens. Do your homework: Go for companies that do more than plant a tree that simply withers. Look for offsets that fund new technologies and send a message to the corporate world and the government.

Meet the Family

It's true, we've asked you to do a whole lot already, and you might need some help with the heavy lifting (always bend your knees). There's no better place to find co-conspirators than your family. Not only can eco-efforts make a difference for the environment, many of them will also save the household money. These are some suggestions for how you and your family can fight climate change together:

Keep the water heater comfy. It may seem bizarre, but your water heater needs a coat. The extra layer will help insulate the hot water, cutting down on energy needed to keep the water toasty and saving up to 1,000 lbs. of CO_2 and $40 per year on your home's energy bill. While you're at it, turn the water heater's top temperature down to 120 degrees Fahrenheit. You'll save an additional 200 lbs. of CO_2 a year for every 20-degree reduction.

Plug those cracks. Insulating your home's attic, pipes, ductwork, and floors can save 25 percent on your energy bill and 2,000 lbs. of CO_2 emissions a year. Don't do this yourself unless your last name is Vila.

In most houses, heating and cooling account for two to three times the amount of energy used for lighting. Work with your family to moderate your space's temperature.

Take two. Moving your heater's thermostat down two degrees in winter and up two degrees in summer saves 2,000 lbs. of CO_2 and roughly $98 per year.

The check's in the email. If all American households went online to view and pay their bills, it would save more than 16 million trees. Encourage your parents to move online with their banking and billing transactions.

Be a star. Replace older appliances with new ones that have Energy Star ratings. Qualified dishwashers use at least 41 percent less energy than the federal minimum standard for energy consumption and much less water. But why stop at the big stuff? Don't forget to use the energy-saving options on all your appliances. Solar-powered nose-hair trimmer, anyone? To learn more about these standards, hit up www.energystar.gov.

MySpace Action

Reach out. Recruit a friend to join the OurPlanet community. Post a new forum topic on www.myspace.com/ourplanet about an environmental issue close to your heart (how hot you think Justin Timberlake is doesn't count). The more active our community is, the more corporate America will listen to our concerns about these important issues.

4. Your Free Time

Get an eco-life

Maybe you thought you could hide from us in the off-hours—when you're out at a concert, seeing a movie, or reading the paper. Nope. We're on to you. You may call it free time, but nothing's really free: Leisure activities can release a significant amount of carbon dioxide and eat up a lot of paper products and energy.

Finding greener ways to amuse ourselves doesn't mean returning to the Stone Age, when the mighty Druids erected great temples from enormous stones, and there weren't . . . even . . . iPods! It's actually pretty easy to make your power- and paper-hungry entertainment more eco-friendly.

Face the Facts

Entertainment life cycles are short. From one-hit wonders to last-year's cell phone model to today's bestseller list, we tend to move from one thing to the next faster than a puppy with ADD. As we move on, we often leave a lot behind.

- Three out of ten consumers who disposed of a TV in the past year dumped their old sets in the trash.

- Nearly 2 in 10 consumers who disposed of desktop computers or monitors in the past year threw them in the trash.

- America's book publishers consume just over a million tons of paper each year for their domestic and international books.

- About 130 million cell phones are retired each year. And 2 in 10 consumers throw their cell phones in the garbage.

Despite these dire statistics, the real concern with entertainment isn't the trash it generates but the energy it consumes. Consumer electronics like DVD players, stereos, and video-game consoles account for about 11 percent of America's residential energy use and 4 percent of the country's overall energy use. In fact, TVs are responsible for about 1 percent of the nation's entire electricity consumption, running up a $4.5 billion electricity bill and causing more than 30 million tons of CO_2 to be emitted from power plants. Time to change the channel?

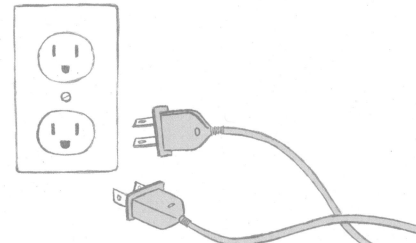

What You Can Do

You can find more eco-friendly ways—both micro and macro—to do your favorite things.

Recharge. How many remotes do you have? (Including the 15 in your couch cushions?) How many batteries does each one take? Around 3 billion batteries are sold in the United States each year—for the equivalent of 10 per person. Unfortunately, batteries are like poison pellets for the environment. They contain toxic heavy metals that can threaten the environment if they're not recycled properly. Buy and use rechargeable batteries wherever possible. When they're worn out, recycle them. To find out where, go to www.rbrc.org. *micro*

Unplug. Unplug it when you're not actively charging your phone. The same goes for all your entertainment gadgets from TVs to CD players to game consoles. *micro*

Plug in. Use a power strip/surge protector for your computer, monitor, printer, and other computer accessories so that the entire strip can be turned off when you're not using your computer and its peripherals. *micro*

Avoid early adoption. Rushing to be the first on your block to get the new PlayStation or the first iPhone may make you look ahead of the curve, but it's not so eco-friendly. Wait until what you already have is ready for a replacement before buying the next new thing. *micro*

Rent or go virtual. Besides the local rental store, consider online music services like iTunes or Rhapsody. Movies and TV shows are also often available for download online, through video-game consoles like the Xbox 360, or through your cable company's on-demand or pay-per-view service. But watch how much electricity you use or your attempts to lessen your material intake will be cancelled out by your energy consumption. *micro*

Put it on your card. You may be surprised at what a library card can get you these days—not just books and magazines but music, DVDs . . . maybe even a laser disc if you're lucky. The library can be an even better choice than the rental store because there's no fee as long as you bring things back on time. *micro*

Sarah
www.myspace.com/vsic
26, Syracuse, NY

It's is all connected, you begin with buying organic produce the next thing you know you are using non-toxic paint for your new home. Local libraries are free and full of eco-friendly books, if you are getting started this is the best place to start.

Be a good sport. When the game's on, make it a party. With fewer TVs on, you're conserving energy. Besides, nachos for one don't taste so great. *micro*

Shoot for the stars. We can roll our eyes all we want, but we have to admit that celebs can have a big influence on eco-awareness. As their fans, you can have a big influence on them. They read the fan sites or have people who do it for them. Tell them what you want them to make the world care about. You'll need strength in numbers to get their attention. *MACRO*

We've touched on the general stuff, so now we can talk specifics.

Tunes

Music's environmental impact isn't limited to noise pollution caused by '80s hair bands and any song with the word "jiggy" in it. From vinyl albums and plastic CD cases to high-tech, high-power recording sessions to massive cross-country tours, music has a major eco-footprint.

Get out of the spin zone. As we shift from disc to download, we throw out literally tons of CDs and jewel cases each year. Unfortunately, recycling all that plastic isn't as easy as recycling an aluminum can. Check out www.greendisk.com for good advice on recycling CDs.

Wrap up well. When you do buy CDs, go for packaging that's made from recycled materials like paper, not plastic.

DIY. Recording your own tracks? When you burn them for your friends, you can make your own cases from a single piece of paper instead of buying a stack of hard or soft plastic cases.

Return to sender. If your MP3 player dies, give it back. Many manufacturers, like Apple, have recycling programs that reuse and recycle parts of their devices and dispose of the toxic parts. Check out www.apple.com/environment/recycling/ for more information.

Go to a green concert. The music industry is waking up to its environmental footprint. Willie Nelson started his own biofuel company to power tour buses in 2004, and other singers like John Mayer, the Beastie Boys, the Fray, and Guster are jumping on the bio-bandwagon.

Watch your waste. Concerts and festivals create mounds of trash. Make sure you toss your trash where it needs to go and recycle what you can.

Do This Right Now

[green] Switch all of your batteries to rechargeable when your current ones die.

[greenest] Make your next concert a green concert. To find one, check out your favorite bands on MySpace. Or buy your tickets from In Ticketing (www.tickomat.net/InTicketing/), an eco-friendly ticketing company.

At the Movies

Hollywood is slowly greening—and by shifting your film-watching habits and educating yourself, you can become just like the movie stars (fame and fortune sold separately).

Support green films. Check out the latest movies from Hollywood studios that are reducing their impact on the climate. Warner was the first Hollywood studio to install a solar-powered electrical system on their main lot. Universal's *Evan Almighty* replaced golf carts and cars with bicycles and recycled as much of the sets as possible. Paramount measured and offset the carbon emissions from *An Inconvenient Truth*, the climate-change documentary with Al Gore. Meanwhile, Twentieth Century Fox (sister company of both HarperCollins and MySpace) is working behind the scenes to make the studio carbon neutral by 2010 and has started using biodiesel generators, solar-powered golf carts, hybrid cars, and more energy-efficient lighting.

Share your popcorn. On average, every man, woman, and child in America consumes 54 quarts of popcorn a year. (Don't forget to floss, Amerca.) Nearly 30 percent is eaten—or spilled—at a place like the movie theater. Next time you order your super-jumbo-trough with extra butter, try sharing it. You might waste less, and make friends.

Watch green films. Beyond Hollywood, there's a whole industry of environmental and nature filmmakers whose work is both educational and entertaining. Many of these are not easily rented at local movie stores or through mail-order movie rentals. To check them out, visit http://greenplanetfilms.org/.

To become an eco-cinéast*, rent:

- *An Inconvenient Truth* (PG): A must watch. If it's even half as bad as Al Gore says it is, we've got work to do.
- *The Day After Tomorrow* (PG-13): All of humanity (played, it seems, by Jake Gyllenhaal) is at risk in this big-budget eco-disaster flick.
- *The Simpsons Movie* (PG-13): What else but climate change would compel Matt Groening and Co. to break out of the small screen?
- *Who Killed the Electric Car?* (PG): Solid documentary about the auto industry's efforts to kill good alternative transportation in its infancy.
- *Erin Brockovich* (R): Julia Roberts portrays this brave whistle-blower in her fight against contaminated drinking water (and the gas company responsible) in her community.
- *Silkwood* (R): The classic corporate whistle-blower story about a corrupt and nefarious nuclear power plant. Exhibit A for why Meryl Streep is the greatest living actress.
- *Syriana* (R): Insanely complex film about oil and terrorism, and the CIA, and some kind of falcon. We promise this movie is incredibly good the second time you watch it.

* snooty word for person who likes movies about the environment

Paper Trail

Even though it seems like we're entirely plugged in, a lot of what we enjoy comes on paper: magazines, books, comics, newspapers, and the backs of cereal boxes. Given how easy it can be to recycle paper, that should be good. But there's more to it than that. To be a better paper consumer:

Buy books like this one. The publishing industry is offering more eco-friendly options. This book's printed on recycled paper using vegetable-based ink. (But please don't try to eat it.)

Avoid trashy books. If your must-read doesn't come on recycled paper, you can still be an eco-reader by sticking to books that can be reused or recycled. Soft-cover books usually can be. Hardcovers for the most part can't be. If you are looking to get rid of books, consider donating them to your local library or school.

Subscribe. Newsstands can be inefficient middlemen when it comes to magazines and newspapers. Although they already have high recycling rates—nearly 70 percent of all newspapers are recycled—you can ensure that your paper or magazine is not wasted and is recycled if you subscribe to it.

For Gamers

If you're a gamer, chances are you spend a lot of time doing what you do. The average full-size game lasts more than 20 hours and that means hours of energy consumed by your console or PC and your TV or computer monitor. It's probably a good idea to consider getting greener energy. (See pp. 37–38.) Other strategies for gaming greener include:

Download. It saves a trip to the game store and zeroes out the effects of packaging. Services like Steam (www.steampowered.com) or Gametap (www.gametap.com) or stores like GameStop (www.gamestop.com) are offering downloadable games for PCs. While consoles don't offer downloading options for full-length games, you can download smaller and classic titles.

Rent. Just like movies, video games can be rented at many movie rental stores as well as through subscription services like Gamefly (www.gamefly.com).

Recycle. More than 150 million consoles and nearly 50 million handheld gaming devices are sold each year—which can generate a lot of gaming garbage. Circuit City maintains a trade-in program and a new initiative from Sony will allow you to recycle all old PlayStations and PSPs at special drop-off locations across the country.

Reuse. Get a pre-owned console, not a new one. When you've beaten them, you can trade in your old games for other gently used titles. Stores like GameStop offer store credit. You can make some extra dough by selling online at eBay (www.ebay.com) or Craigslist (www.craigslist.org), of course. Yes, it turns out someone *will* buy your copy of Sims 2 Pets.

Mark
www.myspace.com/samoanmutt
19, Daytona Beach, FL

Instead of buying regular batteries, get rechargable batteries. They last for over a year and you save a lot of money.

Some More Advice on Eco-friendly Electronics

Buy only what's certifiable. In addition to looking for systems with Energy Star certification, check out the newer EPEAT certification, which evaluates computers and monitors in terms of how they are manufactured, not just how they run.

Save energy, not screens. Screen savers were not developed to cut energy. They were invented to preserve the picture and color quality of a monitor, way back in the '90s when monitors were all cathode ray tubes (C:\dos\run). If you want to save energy, and about $50 a year, it's better to turn your monitor off or put your computer in an idle or "sleep" mode. Even better: Shut your computer down when it's not in use.

Get rid of it responsibly. Transponders. Zip disks. Desktops. Cameras. Laptops. Mice. Ionic hairbrushes. Digital cameras. Death rays. How many do you and your parents have lurking in your junk drawers and in your closets? E-waste is the fastest growing type of garbage in the country. Because of the metal and toxins inside our electronics, e-waste is also some of the hardest garbage to dispose of properly. To find out where to e-cycle your electronics go to www.myspace.com/ourplanet.

The Big Question: Which lullaby should you sing your computer?

Myth: "Sleep mode" automatically saves tons of energy.

Truth: Sleep mode saves some energy, but "standby mode" is more energy efficient. But be aware: You must *choose* to put your computer into standby mode (it's not automatic). As always, shutting it down is the most energy-efficient option.

If you are using a Microsoft operating system, higher versions give you a fourth option: to hibernate. Hibernation is like shutting down the computer because it cuts the energy. But it also allows for a quick start rather than a full reboot—making it the best of both worlds.

Sports

Give your thumbs a rest. You may not know this, but sports-based video games are based on *real live sports*. It's pretty obvious that going to a game or even playing it for real can seem relatively eco-friendly. But there are many ways to make your sporting life even more eco-friendly. Where would you be without us?

When you watch the game:
Don't do it alone. Watching with friends or family is more fun. Plus it can save energy if fewer sets are in use.
Ask yourself if the big screen's really worth it. Plasma TVs are energy hogs and bigger LCD screens burn more energy than small ones.

When you attend the game:
Take the bus or train, carpool, or bike to the game. Many sports arenas and stadiums are connected to local public transportation. Take the train or the bus to and from the game and support not just your team, but our planet. Plus, those parking lots can be a fightmare.
Root for the green team. Some sports teams try to be more eco-friendly than others. For example, the Philadelphia Eagles purchased wind energy credits to cover the power of every home game in their 2007 season. Meanwhile, NASCAR's finally gone unleaded, and Formula 1 has introduced ethanol and hybrid race cars.

When you play sports:
Go eco with your equipment. Use equipment and accessories—like goggle straps and snowboard bags, to name a few—made from recycled, reused, or biodegradable materials. The snowboarding

industry has made the biggest strides here. Check out what they're doing at www.myspace.com/ourplanet.

Drink responsibly. Drinking water is important for your performance. It's also important for our planet for you to drink it in the most eco-friendly way possible. See pp. 21–22 for the pros and cons you should consider when choosing what kind of water to drink.

Some sports are harder on the environment than others. For example, ski resorts use fake snow and energy to heat gondolas and lodges, while golf courses use significant amounts of pesticides, fertilizers, and water. But some sporting associations are acting responsibly to make it easier for you to be an eco-friendly athlete. Check them out on the OurPlanet site.

Good News/Bad News: Photovoltaic Cells

Photovoltaic cells convert sunlight directly into electricity—and they can be used to charge or power small electronic devices like MP3 players, cell phones, and handheld video games. Many companies are combining these solar-power systems with everyday objects like messenger bags and backpacks, flashlights, chargers, and even jackets, allowing you to cleanly charge or power your portable entertainment systems on the go.

How it works: Every day, more energy falls on the United States than we use in an entire year. In fact, it would take the world's 5.9 billion people 27 years to consume the same amount of solar energy that falls on our planet in 24 hours. Photovoltaic cells are designed to capture this energy. The latest inventions sport plugs for charging your gadgets and many of them store energy for a rainy day.

The upside: You get clean, free energy. Plus, you can recharge your batteries even if the electricity goes out.

The downside: Solar power requires sunshine, so charging your charger will require some cooperation from the weather. Plus, many of these solar chargers are still pricey.

Consider solar chargers that have more than one plug-in and that hold a charge so that you can overpower on an overcast day.

Going Green (a real-life story)

Luis Mendoza from Los Angeles, CA, tells this story:

"Last summer the Vans Warped Tour teamed up with EarthEcho International for an Eco Contest to get fans, crew, and sponsors excited about saving the Earth. I was on tour working at the Energizer tent and when I found out about the Eco Contest, I began to think of ways to get fans involved and motivated to recycle. I decided to have fans collect bottles and cans in exchange for a cut pass that enabled them to cut in line for band meet-and-greets. It worked so well that we ended up collecting an average of 300 bottles and cans each day, and more than 800 on a good day, depending on the band.

"I also teamed up with my good friend and began a battery recycling program during the last two weeks of tour. We thought about all the batteries for wireless packs that bands use every single day on tour, and how many of those batteries were ending up in the trash. With the help of the crew on tour, we collected about 400 batteries. Not bad for two weeks. Imagine if we had started this earlier on?"

The Skinny: Television

Televisions account for 1 percent of total U.S. energy consumption. There are, on average, 2.3 televisions per American. TVs are in use far more hours a day now than they were a decade ago. And they tend to have increasingly larger screens—which makes choosing an energy-efficient model much more complicated. Generally, older model TVs that use cathode ray technology (CRT) use more energy than newer models with LCD or projection screens. But new technology isn't always more efficient: Plasma screens gobble up the most energy of any kind of model.

The most eco-friendly choice tends to be a mid-size LCD. Be sure to look for Energy Star models, which save 30 percent more electricity than models without the rating.

A Tree Grows in Hollywood

Ed Begley, Jr.—He might be the greenest guy in Hollywood: He drives an electric car, can fit his garbage in a glove compartment, and put his eco-friendly life in front of the cameras with *Living with Ed*.

George Clooney—He drives the Tango, a mini electric car, and made his movie *Syriana* the first carbon-neutral movie production in Hollywood history.

Ted Danson—He's on the board of Oceana (www.oceana.org), a non-profit that works to protect the world's oceans from pollution and overfishing.

Cameron Diaz—She hosted MTV's eco-oriented show *Trippin'* and was on hand to help Al Gore announce and promote Live Earth. www.myspace.com/current_ecospot

Leonardo DiCaprio—He produced *The 11th Hour* and is a board member of the Natural Resources Defense Council. www.myspace.com/leonardodicaprio

Matt Groening/Lisa Simpson—The creator of *The Simpsons* decided Homer should work in a nuclear plant so the show could frequently return to issues of energy and toxic waste, while Lisa Simpson has become the most eco-aware cartoon character in history.

Daryl Hannah—She's driven across America in her "frybrid"—a 1983 El Camino fueled by biodiesel and vegetable oil—to promote biofuels. We admit it: We might have a little crush.

Woody Harrelson—Not only does he live on a commune in Hawaii, drive a biofuel car, and grow the majority of his own food, he co-founded, with his wife, the website Voice Yourself (www.voiceyourself.com) to help others "live lightly."

MySpace Action

Befriend the Glitterati. Many celebrities, sports figures, and entertainment stars have MySpace profiles. Leave them comments encouraging them to use their high profile to promote environmental causes. Or, friend celebrities known to be eco-friendly, and leave them a friendly shout-out.

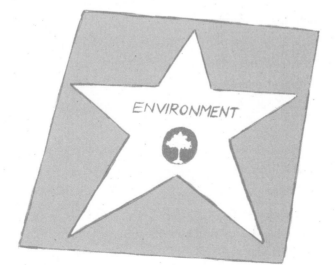

ENVIRONMENT

5. Social Life

Gift Responsibly

With the exception of our crazy uncle Herbie, we love the holidays—or any chance we have to spend time with friends and family. You probably feel the same way (you'd feel the same way about Uncle Herbie if you met him). For all of us, holidays and special occasions are a time to splurge—on food, gifts, decorations, and activities. But while we think of them as unchangeable traditions—what would the Fourth of July be without the fireworks?—there are a number of ways we can make the good times greener.

Face the Facts

All this celebrating affects not only your social life, but our planet—and often in adverse ways. While you're partying, the environment may be suffering:

- Americans purchase around 7 billion greeting cards each year. If none of them contained any recycled paper, that would mean that more than 2.5 million trees were chopped down to produce them.

- Between Thanksgiving and New Year's, Americans throw away nearly 2 billion lbs. more garbage a week than they do at other times during the year.

- Holiday gift buying is the top category that Americans feel they overspend on each year.

What You Can Do

It's possible to celebrate a greener birthday, a greener holiday season, or an eco-friendly alternative spring break by making a few changes.

Give a gift they really want. Put down the fruitcake. Unhand the garden gnome. Stop walking around aimlessly in the mall waiting for inspiration or filling your basket with random crapola that will just wind up in the garbage. Ask what your family and friends want. Consult any online "wish lists." Consider an electronic gift card to their favorite store. *micro*

Skip the paper card. Try an e-card. If you do buy a paper card, look for cards that are 100 percent post-consumer recycled (PCR) or have been processed chlorine free (PCF). *micro*

Get some new(s) wrapping. Most wrapping paper is not recyclable, and neither is ribbon. One abundant alternative wrapping paper is newsprint. Also consider cloth or brown paper bags. Save ribbons you receive yourself and use them to smarten up your eco-friendly wrapping. *micro*

Let them eat cake on real plates. The clean-up might take longer, but using regular china rather than paper or plastic plates will mean less garbage and less environmental impact. If you do use plastic plates and cups consider washing and reusing them since they can't be recycled. Or spring for biodegradable bamboo or corn- or potato-based "plastic." *micro*

Make sure there's some takeaway. What's a holiday without eating . . . and overeating? Plan for the leftovers to go home with the guests. It'll save a lot of food from being wasted and prevent your having to eat turkey and cranberry sandwiches in the second week of December. What can't be put in doggie bags can be composted. *micro*

Eco-decorate. Instead of hanging paper streamers, string LED lights in your houseplants. Instead of party hats, reuse bows and ribbons you have gotten in the past and create your own headpiece. When it comes to the holidays, don't buy new decorations every year. Invest in reusable, vintage, or homemade items. *micro*

Go on an alternative spring break. The beach is relaxing, but it may have been built with lax environmental codes. So rather than lying on an eroding stretch of sand, go for an eco-friendly option. Volunteer to clean up a local stream that's been polluted. Help renovate an inner-city school to make it more environmentally friendly. *micro*

Celebrate without conspicuous consumption. Suggest to your family or friends that you make the upcoming holiday or get-together less about consumption and more about community. Combine the micro tips so that you have a party, but not a big fat waste-fest. *MACRO*

☺☺☺Anuva☺☺☺
www.myspace.com/anuvak
16, Candy, CA

*If you're going to a party and so are your friedns, carpool . . .
save gas and start having fun before you even reach*

Jules
www.myspace.com/245695691
30, Chicago, IL

*I reuse my take out cartons to store left over food. I reuse
bread bags as my zip lock bags. Granted my bread bags don't
have the "yellow and blue make green" but by reusing them
essentially I am making green!*

Happy Holidays

You can be eco-friendly throughout the year. Start with the ideas below, and then think of your own eco-friendly fixes for all your other favorite holidays.

Valentine's Day
- Say "be mine" with a plant rather than roses, which will wilt.
- Choose chocolate that's organic.

July 4th
- Pack your picnic with reusable or recyclable containers.
- Skip the frozen desserts and have the fresh fruit that's in season.
- Avoid buying your personal stash of fireworks. It's greener—and safer—to enjoy fireworks provided by your town. You may also save money on hand-reattachment surgery.

Halloween
- Don't buy a cheap pre-packaged outfit. Rent a costume (make sure it passes the smell test, of course) or create your own.

Thanksgiving
- Whether or not you've successfully convinced your family to eat more organic food (see p. 13 for more information), suggest an organic turkey. After all, it's the centerpiece of the meal.
- If you're going to watch football, don't leave the game on all day.

New Year's
- Make your resolutions eco-friendly, not just the usual "I'm finally going to ask her out." Just ask her out already, and get to the important stuff.

Dreaming of a Green Christmas

No other holiday has as much exuberant excess and as many gift exchanges as Christmas. But you can begin to celebrate in less extravagant, more eco-friendly ways:

- **Investigate the roots.** If your family has a yard and you live in the right climate, you can get a planted Christmas tree this season and have it year-round. But if you get one of the 30 to 35 million real Christmas trees that are sold every year in the United States, make sure the tree is recycled.

  To find out where to recycle your family's Christmas tree, contact your town's department of sanitation, department of parks and recreation, or the mayor's office. Also, use your zip code in the recycling search at www.earth911.org.

- **String the tree with LED lights.** Rather than using traditional strings of incandescent lights, consider using LED lights. Added bonus: They use about a tenth of the energy of conventional lights and, since they produce no heat, present little fire risk.

- **Have a less lonely holiday season by carpooling.** You travel more during the holiday season—to the mall, to parties, to relatives' houses. If each person reduced their holiday gas consumption by one gallon, we could reduce CO_2 emissions by 6 billion lbs. And it's always greener to take public transportation.

Good News/Bad News: Making It a Mail-Order Holiday

Ordering gifts online is supposedly more eco-friendly than trekking out to the mall. It does mean you'll be driving less, but it doesn't necessarily mean the same is true for your gifts.

The rationale: You expend a lot of energy going to the store to buy the perfect gift (we want a pony). To cut down on your emissions, you order the perfect gift online and let it come to you. By bypassing the local store, your purchase arrives more efficiently, burning less fuel.

The upside: Many online retailers let you choose to have all of your items sent together rather than as soon as they're in stock. This can cut down on packaging.

The downside: If you bike or walk to the store, ordering online may not be the most eco-friendly option. Worse, if no one's home to get a package, your purchase may make more trips than you anticipate—and you get those annoying "we came, we left" notices, which waste paper.

Consider: Factor all the options into your situation. The shipping industry's carbon footprint as a whole is 600 million tons, which is higher than Canada's total annual CO_2 emissions. However, shippers are making efforts to green their fleets by investing in hybrid and alternative-fuel vehicles. UPS has invested in GPS software that takes their trucks on right-turn only routes in high volume areas to avoid idling and save gas. And some eco-retailers are using shipping services that offset the CO_2 emissions of shipping a purchase. For a list of eco-retailers that offset emissions, check out www.carbonfund.org.

Birthdays

Another year older, and now a little bit greener.

Huff and puff, but only if it's soy. Candles are typically made out of paraffin—which comes from petroleum. Replace them with candles made from soy. Otherwise you may want to hold your breath and your wish till next year.

Have we mentioned recycling? (Yes, we have.) The majority of everyday greeting cards sold each year are birthday cards, and if you're like most Americans, birthday cards make up about a third of all the cards you receive each year. Be sure to recycle those well wishes (just don't tell Grandma—as far as she's concerned, you save *everything* she sends you).

Get a receipt. If there's a chance you may not use a gift, ask if there's a gift receipt in the box. Or, at the very least, find out where it was purchased. Consider returning it or exchanging it for something you will use.

Sheri
www.myspace.com/sweetsheri3
15, Sylmar, CA

Send E-cards for the holidays instead of sending cards by mail. There are a lot of great & creative E-cards online.

Gifts

By this point, you know how to celebrate the holidays in a green way. Here are some pointers to help you pick the right gift.

Give eco-gifts. Consider giving your relatives and buddies a gift that will help them live in a more eco-friendly fashion. Something as simple as a stylish reusable bag or water bottle is also a gift to the planet.

Think outside the box. Go alternative and give a renewable energy card. It will help reduce global warming by keeping a ton of CO_2 out of the atmosphere by replacing energy from fossils with energy from renewable sources (Try: www.nativeenergy.com). Or make a donation that supports sustainable development in the developing world (www.alternativegifts.com or www.heifer.org). Or give a micro-loan to someone in need (www.kiva.org). Not only will you help others, it's a gift that gives back.

The 3 R's of Gift-giving

Repurpose. You can reuse greeting cards by cutting them up to make gift tags. Just be sure they're eventually recycled.

Rewrap. Take a cue from the Japanese custom of *furoshiki* and wrap your gifts in cloth. It saves paper and means your wrapping paper can be reused. And if you're crafty, it means your gift can count as a two-fer. Scarves and hand towels can make unique wrappings.

Re-gift. Everyone does it, and it turns out it can be eco-friendly, too. Just try not to re-gift to the same person who gave you the gift. That could be awkward.

Prom

With these eco-friendly moves, you can be the greenest cat on the dance floor.

Pretend you're a movie star. Instead of renting a limo, take a cue from the 2007 Academy Awards and rent a hybrid.

Don't go alone. Whatever you do, make sure you ride with others to the big event.

Do it in the dark. What?! We didn't specify what "it" is! Get your mind out of the gutter. Yeesh . . . Save electricity by turning the lights down low.

Do This Right Now

[green] Give a green gift—and use a green alternative to traditional wrapping paper.

[greener] At your next party, make it a goal to have a bigger bag of recyclables than garbage.

[greenest] Do your holiday shopping in one trip.

Eco-dating

We're always attracted to people who share our values and ideals. So if your commitment to the environment matters to you, chances are you'll want your relationships to look and feel eco-friendly, too. Eco-dating can actually be a great way to get to know someone while doing something good for the planet. Skip the standard dinner and a movie, and spend a few hours together biking, hiking, or even doing cleanup or preservation work in a nearby park or green space. You'll get to know more about each other than you would if you were sitting in a movie theater, anyway. Need a new outfit for a date? Check a thrift store for a recycled outfit instead of shopping at the mall. Bringing flowers? Look for locally grown organic flowers, instead of roses shipped from Europe or South America. Green-lighted for a second date? Surprise your eco-sweetheart with a well-planned eco-date that includes use of public transportation, a picnic or homemade organic meal, and a nature walk into the sunset together!

Take a Break

As far as we're concerned, there are no more important yearly events than winter, spring, and summer breaks. In choosing how to spend them, there are several basic ways you can make them more eco-friendly.

Eco-tour. Eco-tourism is a growing industry and can let you see more of the world with less of the guilt. See p. 78 for tips on how to green your travel.

Break for a change. Instead of sleeping in, get energized by using your break to get a green job or internship. Work at an eco-camp. Intern with the Natural Resources Defense Council (www.nrdc.org) or another environmentally focused non-profit. Look on your favorite group's website to see what kind of internship opportunities they offer.

Volunteer as a group. Organize a group of your green friends to team up with a local organization or environmental non-profit. You can work together to tackle a community project they've been meaning to complete.

For more on volunteering, visit the search tool powered by VolunteerMatch at www.myspace.com/volunteerspace.

The Skinny:
Alternative Spring Break

Using your free time for community service is not a new idea. But turning your spring break—a vacation with a raucous reputation—into a coordinated trip to help others is a fairly new trend. Over the last decade, tens of thousands of students from high schools and colleges around the country have gone on an alternative spring break (ASB) and made a difference in communities nationwide and around the globe. Not all of them target environmental issues, of course. But you can take the lead in organizing an alternative spring break with a green theme. For advice and ideas:

The leader in advising and coordinating alternative spring breaks is Break Away: www.alternativebreaks.org

The Charity Guide offers a list of ideas on environmental vacations you can take: www.charityguide.org/volunteer/vacation/topic/environmental-protection.htm

Vacation!

When it comes to how we treat the environment, American families seem to be on a break from even their smallest eco-friendly efforts. The average hotel, for example, consumes more than 200 gallons of water per occupied hotel room each day—nearly equal to the amount a typical U.S. household uses daily. So get your family and friends to follow an eco-friendly itinerary.

Go online before you go out. Use online guidebooks and maps. Print out only what you need—and be sure to recycle that paper when you're back home.

Rent a hybrid. Mainstream car-rental companies like Avis, Enterprise Rent-a-Car, and Hertz have begun adding thousands of hybrids to their fleets, and smaller companies like EV Rental Cars (www.evrental.com) in Los Angeles have hybrid-only fleets. Even if you don't want to rent, look into eco-oriented car services in bigger cities like New York (www.ozocar.com) and Los Angeles (www.evolimo.com).

Say cheese. Don't use disposable cameras. Go digital. You can save waste and upload your pics to your MySpace profile easy-breezy.

Pick the right hotel environment. Hotels and hostels are choosing eco-friendly operations, whether by adopting a linen-reuse policy, using greener energy like solar power, or fitting organic sheets on their beds. Visit www.greenhotels.com or www.hostelworld.com to find a greener place to stay.

6. On the Road

Rethink Your Wheels

America may be driving the climate crisis. Literally. We use a disproportional amount of energy—about a quarter of the world's energy resources—despite having less than 5 percent of the world's population. A lot of that energy—around 70 percent of our oil consumption, in fact—is spent on transportation.

All that movement is expensive. We spend more than $200,000 per minute and around $13 million per hour on foreign oil. But all those trips aren't just draining our wallets. They're draining the world's oil reserves and filling our atmosphere with carbon dioxide—the main cause of global warming and the main driver of climate change.

Face the Facts

- Trains, planes, and automobiles may be the fastest ways to get where you need to go, but they're usually the worst for the environment.

- The average American emits more than 20 metric tons of CO_2 per year. Compare that to the rest of the world population, which emits an average of 4 tons per person. A third of this is from travel.

- Gasoline-guzzling vehicles are the second largest source of our CO_2 emissions, with the average car producing 20 lbs. of CO_2 for every gallon of gas it uses.

What You Can Do

Feet first. Use your feet to walk, pedal, and skate your way from here to there. You will reduce your carbon footprint by 1 lb. for every mile you don't drive. *micro*

Go public. Use public transportation, such as subways, buses, and light-rail networks where it's available. Because they're concentrated in urban areas plagued by traffic snarls, these public networks can make your trip faster and less enraging. *micro*

Travel in herds. Moo. When you travel with others—be it in a car or taxi or on the bus or subway—you increase your fuel efficiency. In fact, the average bus has a higher fuel efficiency with only seven passengers than the average commuter has driving alone. *micro*

Slow down. Nearly every car's fuel efficiency goes down at speeds over 60 mph, meaning you're using more gas less efficiently and reducing your car's overall efficiency. Although different size cars use different amounts of energy at the same speed, you can assume that for every 5 mph you drive over 60 mph, you're paying an additional $0.20 per gallon of gas. *micro*

Ramp up your mpgs. Double your gas mileage and you cut emissions by half. Also, get more gas for your money: The difference between a car that gets 20 mpg (miles per gallon) and one that gets 30 mpg amounts to $744 per year (assuming an average of 15,000 miles per year and a fuel cost of $2.97—always read the fine print). *micro*

Fly only when you must. Air travel is increasingly popular. It's also increasingly responsible for more and more air pollution at higher and higher altitudes. One cross-country flight from New York to Los Angeles emits 1 ton of CO_2 per passenger. Take the train for trips less than 500 miles. It will save 310 lbs. of CO_2—and may take less time. **micro**

Don't forget to pack. Take your eco-friendly habits with you when you go on vacation. Look into eco-friendly hotels. Stay in central locations so you can walk, bike, or take public transportation. **micro**

Travel in neutral. You can be carbon neutral by offsetting your auto and plane emissions. Just don't use offsetting as an excuse for not reducing your miles. Offsetting doesn't prevent oil resources from being used. It also doesn't decrease the amount of other pollutants like nitrogen oxides, hydrocarbons, and particulate matter that your car releases. (See pp. 40–41 to learn more about what "neutral" means and how to choose a reputable carbon offsetter.) **MACRO**

kaitlin :] !
www.myspace.com/kaitlinkayyy
14, Long Beach, CA

I take the bus to school, and not only do I save gas and reduce emissions, I save money. Most citys have buses to take and its a great way to help the enviroment. If everyone took the bus, the emissions would be reduced greatly. also, many citys are making there buses electric which is even better! we have to help the earth one day at a time, and even the small things count.

Miceli<3
www.myspace.com/rachlie
15, Florida

Take the bus. It is a simple way to save gas and it causes less air pollution. The more people who take buses, the less cars that will be driving in the mourning when they dont need to be, and the less the better. By getting more vehicles off the road you could slow down Global warming.

Mj
www.myspace.com/mjane
23, Fresno, CA

Instead of driving back and forth from place to place i get everything done at once, i even take my bike when i can and my friends have caught on!!!

Use these tips to become eco-friendly in all the ways you travel from here to there.

We Like Bikes

Why, you ask? *They don't emit CO_2.* The United States could save about 460 million gallons of gas each year if Americans increased the number of trips they biked from 1 percent to 1.5 percent.

Short is sweet. Because a cold engine has to work harder, short car trips create more pollution and release nearly three times more CO_2 than longer trips. Choosing to bike rather than drive these short distances will prevent 3.6 lbs. of auto pollution per mile.

Pedal on. Biking isn't just an alternative for short neighborhood trips. It's possible to bike the long haul if you know where you're going. You can find detailed maps designed for bike riders for sale at www.adventurecycling.com.

Power up. Even motorized two wheels are better than four. A motorized bike or scooter uses less CO_2 and may be worth it if you tend not to bike because you're tired of pedaling.

Public Transportation

Fourteen million Americans take public transportation daily. Get on the bus . . . or train.

De-smog. Public transportation prevents the emission of 126 million lbs. of hydrocarbons, the primary cause of smog.

More bang for the buck. Full buses are 6 times more fuel efficient than cars with one occupant; full rail cars are 15 times more efficient.

Save gas and cut emissions. Public transportation usage reduces annual gasoline consumption by 1.4 billion gallons in the United States. That's equal to 108 million cars filling up.

Avoid traffic. Americans spent 3.7 billion hours in traffic in 2003. That's a statistic we definitely don't want to be a part of!

Car Talk

If you can't imagine life without your car, you're not alone. Although the United States makes up less than 5 percent of the world's population, Americans own one-third of the world's cars. Think about going carless. You could start a trend. Meanwhile, here are some ways to decrease your car's harm to our planet.

Don't idle. It's true that starting your engine uses more energy than it takes to run it. But idling for more than a minute uses even more energy. So turn it off if you want to emit less CO_2.

Accelerate gradually. Quick stops and starts use more energy and wear out your brakes. When possible use cruise control to stay at steady speeds on the highway.

Open the windows in traffic. Running the AC uses more energy and creates more air pollutants.

Use your AC on the highway. Opening the window while driving at high speeds creates drag and decreases your fuel efficiency, so if opening the vents is not cool enough, turn the AC on.

Get regular tune-ups. A badly tuned car uses almost 10 percent more gas than a well-tuned car, so make sure you change your oil and air filter and have the wheels rotated and aligned regularly. Also check for worn tires and spark plugs.

Keep your tires properly pumped up. Keeping tires inflated to their recommended level improves fuel efficiency by around 3 percent. When you replace tires, buy new ones that will give you the highest mileage.

Lighten your load. Driving a lighter car or clearing out your trunk will raise your mpgs by up to 2 percent per 100 lbs.

Go short-term. Book short-term car rentals (www.zipcar.com or www.flexcar.com) or participate in local car-sharing options (like www.citycarshare.org in the Bay Area).

Find out how your car stacks up on fuel efficiency by going to www.epa.gov/greenvehicles/.

Change Your Oil . . . Company

Even the most eco-conscious drivers have to fill up. Choosing which oil company to buy your gas from can be agonizing. Fortunately, some of these mega-villains of environmentalism have been cleaning up their acts in recent years—and it's not all smog and mirrors. The Sierra Club recently evaluated the top eight U.S. oil companies, which together reap more than $1.4 trillion in sales. The resulting environmentalist's guide to gasoline—an admittedly subjective project—ranked these energy behemoths from the bottom of the barrel (ExxonMobil and ConocoPhillips) to the top (BP and Sunoco), depending on their corporate attitudes and attentiveness to the environment. For more information on these ratings and why they matter, go to www.myspace.com/sierraclubnational.

The Big Question: Hybrids v. Conventional Engines

Driving a fuel-efficient hybrid can save you 16,000 lbs. of CO_2 and close to $4,000 per year. Plus, as hybrid technology improves, the prospects only increase for how eco-friendly these cars will be. But is driving a hybrid the only way to really be more eco-friendly on four wheels?

Myth: Hybrids are the antidote to our seemingly bottomless appetite for oil.

Truth: Hybrids accounted for 200,000 new car sales in 2005. That's 1.2 percent of the 17 million cars sold that year. Even if every new hybrid owner saved a gallon of gas a day, that would save a mere

200,000 gallons—taking the daily U.S. gas consumption rate from 400,000,000 to 399,800,000 gallons.

Impressive? Not so much. But if all those conventional gasoline-fueled cars increased their fuel efficiency from today's rough average of 25 mpg to 45 mpg, we'd eliminate our dependence on foreign oil. By comparison, if each driver biked rather than drove 5 to 10 miles a day or went carless one day a week, we'd not only save about 400 million gallons, but we'd also eliminate our CO_2 output by 416 billion lbs. a year.

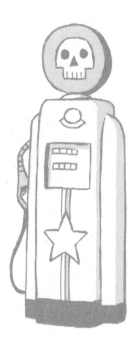

For more information on how hybrids work, visit www.hybridcenter.org.

Going Green (a real-life story)

In 2005, West Philadelphia High School's Electric Vehicle Team did something that Honda and Toyota couldn't do: They won the Tour de Sol, the nation's premiere alternative-fuel-vehicle competition. The students from this inner-city high school built their biodiesel "Hybrid Attack" from a car kit and a turbo-diesel Volkswagen engine. The Hybrid Attack beat out the competition from major car companies, alternative-fuel entrepreneurs, and college and university teams by getting 50 mpg, boasting over 300 horsepower, and going from 0 to 60 in less than 4 seconds. A "muscle" hybrid, the Attack's electric motor was used mostly for acceleration. But its fuel efficiency leaves even the Toyota Prius in the dust.

The Skinny: Alternative Fuels

A hybrid isn't the only choice you have when it comes to making your car run cleaner and greener. By feeding your car from the growing menu of alternative fuels, you can release less CO_2 into the air than you would using conventional gasoline. Just make sure your car can digest what you're feeding it.

Biofuel (ethanol)—A biofuel is made from plants. Currently the most popular biofuel is ethanol, which is made from corn kernels. Biofuels, if developed and manufactured in eco-friendly ways, can potentially cut U.S. greenhouse gas emissions by 1.7 billion tons per year by 2050. That would reduce our transportation-related emissions by more than 80 percent.

Ethanol can be used in "flex-fuel" cars, and many cars on the road today are already designed for flex-fuel options. To check a car's flex-fuel status, go to www.e85fuel.com/e85101/flexfuelvehicles.php.

Biodiesel—Biodiesel is a renewable, biodegradable fuel made from vegetable oils like soybean or corn oil or animal fats. It is usually mixed with diesel to create a biodiesel blend. It burns cleaner than fossil-fuel diesel and is considered carbon neutral because the carbon it releases is absorbable by the plants the fuel was originally created from.

Biodiesel can fuel most diesel engines without modification. You can modify diesel cars to create "frybrids," which use common vegetable oil and are filled up by local restaurants from their cooking and frying waste.

Natural gas—Natural gas is a combustible mixture of hydrocarbon gases, and in its compressed form, it can fuel specially designed internal combustion engines in cars. Unlike gasoline, it is gaseous in form.

Natural-gas cars are not widely available to consumers, although they are used in public transportation and government fleets. There are fewer than 1,000 natural gas stations in the United States. (Sigh.)

To find out where to fuel up using alternative fuels, visit: http://afdcmap2.nrel.gov/locator/

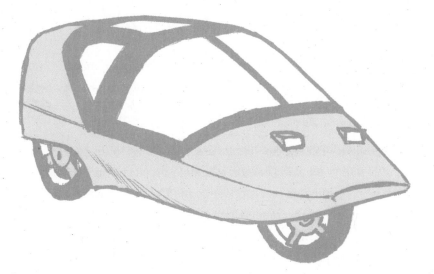

Do This Right Now

[green] Walk or bike one trip a week that you normally would have driven.

[greener] Drive the speed limit for a week.

[greenest] Shave 5 miles off your driving time each day this week, or go car-free for an entire day. If every American driver reduced average daily driving by just 5 miles, it would save 50 million gallons of gas every day.

Good News/Bad News: Biofuels

Flex-fuel seems like a clean, sure way to make driving more environmentally friendly. But not everyone's onboard when it comes to biofuel. Why?

The upside: Biofuels like ethanol are considered to be carbon neutral due to a natural carbon offsetting process: The CO_2 they emit when burned as fuel is offset by the CO_2 they absorbed as they were grown. This means that, unlike fossil fuels, they don't add carbon to the system. Plus, they're renewable and homegrown.

The downside: While they're better in terms of emissions, corn-fed cars don't reliably produce better gas mileage. In fact, it's usually less. Concerns have also grown over whether growing crops like corn for the fuel market rather than the supermarket will drive up their price, making it harder for poorer people to buy staple foods made from corn. Also, growing and harvesting biofuels can use vast amounts of water and energy and fertilizers.

Consider: Frybrids. Modifying cars to recycle cooking oils from local restaurants will void the manufacturer's warranty. But that may not matter if you're converting a 20-year-old diesel dinosaur that's years past its warranty into a green machine.

What's next: In Brazil, ethanol is made from sugar. And second-generation biofuels made not from corn but "cellulosic" waste from grass plants like switchgrass are being developed. Think of it as an "alternative alternative" fuel.

jeanette
www.myspace.com/jeanetteisworking
27, Toledo, OH

I like to irritate people on the highway by setting my cruise control at an efficient 55mph. I also grab the bus when it's convenient, which isn't often in my city. And when the weather's nice, there's nothing better than traveling via bicycle.

Indy Sioux Soldier
www.myspace.com/gofightingsioux
100, CA

Study's have shown that Airplanes use 8 times as much Oil based fuels than trains. So the next time you want to travel take a train see what nature has to offer along the way.

Do This Right Now

[green] Drive a hybrid.

[greener] Take the bus.

[greenest] Ride a bike.

MySpace Action

Shake up your routine and share it with the world! Post a video of you and your friends walking, biking, or taking public transportation instead of driving to school, your job, or your favorite hangout. Chances are, the fun you have together could inspire some of your MySpace friends to try the same thing (and, like Mom always says, imitation is the sincerest form of flattery . . .).

7. Money— the Original "Green"

Spending Smart

If we could shop our way to a greener world, Americans would be leading the charge to prevent global warming. That is not exactly the case (yet) but it is still possible for us to align our shopping habits with our eco-driven values. The trick is finding the right balance between reducing the amount of stuff you consume and going greener with every purchase.

Face the Facts

The never-ending life cycle of the American consumer: We buy, we use, we toss. But there, in the trash, then in the dump or landfill, our discarded crap lives on and on and on. The first step in making your shopping environmentally friendlier is thinking about where a product came from, how it got to you, and where it will go after you bid it farewell.

- Americans spend an average of 24 minutes a day shopping.
- We make about 127 million trips each week to Wal-Mart alone.
- In America, manufacturing and industrial facilities produce about 7.6 billion tons of solid waste each year.

What You Can Do

You can make your shopping more eco-friendly by making micro changes as well as macro ones. Here is a checklist:

❏ **Want not, waste not.** Wait a day or 10 between deciding you want something and actually laying down the dough for it. *micro*

❏ **Pile in.** Carpool with friends and combine trips to the store. Better yet—bike or walk to the store whenever you can. *micro*

❏ **Judge your next purchase by what it comes in, not just what's inside.** Buy products with less packaging to cut down on waste. Choose to have all items sent in one shipment if you order online. *micro*

❏ **BYOB(ag). It's the greener answer to "Paper or plastic?"** By taking a reusable canvas or cloth tote to the store and reusing it, you will cut down on the waste that comes from the 10 billion paper bags and more than 500 billion plastic bags used each year. *micro*

❏ **"Paper or plastic?" part 2.** If you are thinking of getting a credit card, sign up with a service that makes the environment a priority. *micro*

❏ **Help yourself to seconds.** Shop or barter for used gear at secondhand stores, online at websites like Craigslist, eBay, and Freecycle.com, or at swapping parties. *micro*

❏ **Give green to green.** When you do buy, support businesses that are ecologically aware. *MACRO*

Dudley, sweet and tender hooligan
www.myspace.com/smiths
26, Valencia, CA

Whenever you go to the ATM or have a choice about getting a receipt, don't. These days you can check all of your transactions online and the need for a hard copy of a receipt is unnecessary.

Come To Mama Vintage
www.myspace.com/cometomamavintage
44, Silverlake, CA

We stopped using bags in my vintage clothing shop almost 1 year ago and instead wrap merchandise in vintage scarves & ribbons & bits that can again & again be used as giftwrap. Everybody wins! :)

Nikki
www.myspace.com/janikki
16, California

Swap clothes with a friend instead of buying more. It helps reduce the carbon dioxide produced during production and transportation. Looking hot shouldn't make the planet any hotter!

To deepen the impact of your shopping decisions, use these tips.

Shop Right

Swap, don't shop. Invite your best-dressed (and similarly sized) friends to a swapping party. This can be done with video games and books if, like us, you only wear Hello Kitty sweaters *all the time*.

Buy cleaner clothes. We've mentioned this already, but it's worth reiterating. Think twice before buying clothes that need dry cleaning. Sure, you won't have to fold them, but besides costing you more, dry cleaning typically uses perchloroethylene, or PERC, a solvent that is toxic to humans and a key ingredient in smog. If you must dry-clean, find a store that uses Green Earth or other eco-conscious methods, such as wetcleaning with liquid carbon dioxide. More at: www.greenearthcleaning.com.

Sold on recycled soles. Your bulky shoes take up a lot of space in the bottom of your closet. Guess what? They do exactly the same thing in our landfills. But because of their sturdy function and form, soles can easily be made from recycled materials like wood, plastic, and rubber tires. Look for these when you need new shoes.

Supplies

Nearly every type of school supply comes in a recycled format, particularly if it has paper or certain kinds of plastic in it. Look for recycled materials when you buy these basics.

- Spiral and bound notebooks
- File folders
- Sticky notes
- Binders
- Rulers
- Tape dispensers

Food

Eat local, fresh, and organic. Frozen food uses 10 times more energy to produce than fresh food. By eating local and organic foods, you reduce the emissions associated with transport and chemical production. You can find local food vendors at www.foodroutes.org.

Be conscious of food containers. They're rarely made from biodegradable or recycled material. Avoid excessive packaging.

Lighten the to-go bag. When you order takeout, tell them to keep the stack of napkins and ask for just one. The same goes for utensils.

See pp. 15–17 for more on eco-friendly food choices.

Household Goods

You may not be in charge of most of your household purchases, but put these on your family's shopping list if you can:

Recycled toilet paper. It may not be as soft, but it will mean you're flushing away fewer virgin trees. (It's *recycled*, not reused.) And if every household in America bought a 12-pack of 100 percent recycled paper rather than 400-sheet rolls made from virgin fiber, it would save 4.4 million trees and prevent the equivalent of 17,000 garbage trucks full of TP from going to a landfill.

Recycled or biodegradable trash bags. You've heard it takes 500 years for a plastic bag to degrade. That may or may not be true—plastic bags have been around only about 50 years—but we do know that throwing away plastic isn't the same as throwing away a banana peel. (It isn't as funny, either.) Choose trash bags made from recycled post- and pre-consumer plastic or bags made from biodegradable sources like corn or potatoes.

Buy in bulk. Usually it can cut down on packaging and will save your family money. This also means going for the gallon—or whatever is the bigger size—with items like milk or other groceries. Substituting bigger containers will allow you to buy fewer smaller items, trimming the amount of packaging you're paying for and throwing away.

An Eco-Friendly Shopping List

You're going to buy them anyway, so make sure the green option is on your list:

- Rechargeable batteries (Why? See p. 46)
- Recycled paper products (Why? See p. 33)
- A refillable water bottle (Why? See pp. 21–22)
- Compact fluorescent bulbs (Why? See p. 26)

But be sure to cross these items off your list:

- Bottled water (Why? See pp. 21–22)
- Disposable products (Why? See pp. 11–12)
- Anything made of Styrofoam. Why? Styrofoam, which generically is known as polystyrene, is not easily recyclable. Avoid products made from it. If you received a package filled with polystyrene "peanuts," you can return them to packaging stores or manufacturers. Call the Peanut Hotline (800-828-2214) or check out this list of drop-off locations: www.epspackaging.org/info.html.

Good News/Bad News: Organic Clothes

Organic clothing may be where recycled paper was a decade ago—a growing business that's a little spotty on quality poised on the verge of hitting the mainstream. Plus, most organic clothing tends to be boutique—trendy and high-end. But the quality is changing as new materials are being introduced—bamboo underwear, anyone? Even mainstream retailers will soon have an organic store near you. Case in point: In 2006, Wal-Mart became the largest single buyer of 100 percent organic cotton products in the world.

How it works: What makes organic clothes organic? Chemical pesticides and fertilizers are not used in the cotton farming process.

The upside: Fabric production is an environmentally intensive process. With organic fabric, you are at least guaranteeing that fewer chemicals—particularly pesticides and fertilizers—were used in creating them.

The downside: Organic farming can lead to more expensive fabrics, though it doesn't have to: Wal-Mart's initiatives are aimed at low-cost options, even for organic clothing. No organic certification process exists for many eco-fabrics made from crops like bamboo and hemp, so it's hard to be sure you're really buying organic. Also, organic cotton is still a water-intensive crop, meaning its environmental impact remains high.

Consider splurging on: Jeans made from organic cotton. Yes, a lot of water was used in growing the cotton. But you probably wear jeans more than any other type of clothing, so why not go eco? Even mainstream brands like Levi's are offering organic options.

The Big Question: Paper or Plastic?

Myth: Plastics: They're strong, they don't break, they last forever— and they make up most of the municipal solid waste in this country.

Truth: It's true that plastics are durable, but by weight, *paper* makes up 35 percent of our garbage. Plastic takes up a mere 11 percent. However, plastic chews up a lot of volume, which is why we should recycle as much of it as we can.

To find out whether that plastic jug or Power Rangers action figure can be recycled, look for its number, which should be in a small triangular recycling symbol on the bottom, and see if your local recycling facilities will accept that type.

Myth: Paper bags are better than plastic bags.

Truth: Paper bags may look more natural, may have a higher chance of being recycled, and typically hold more. But paper bags aren't as environmentally friendly as they seem. They usually require virgin, rather than recycled pulp. Paper manufacturers consume more fresh water than any other industry on the planet. That's why it's best to choose a reusable canvas or cloth bag.

Don't Be Greenwashed

As more and more people pay attention to the looming climate crisis, corporate America is noticing the environment's marketing power. They're plastering their products with words like "natural" and "green," sunrise seals, and green-hued logos, hoping to appeal to you, the eco-friendly consumer. It can be hard to pinpoint what truth there is in this advertising—some companies are undoubtedly using these labels as a fig leaf to cover their less-than-sustainable manufacturing. That's why it's important to be skeptical before you buy. Do a little research about what you're buying and the history of the company that made it.

The Eco-Shopping Quiz:

Asking yourself these simple questions each time you shop will help make your purchase more eco-friendly:

- Do I need this?
- Where was it made?
- What is it made from?
- How is it packaged?
- What will I do with it when I've used/worn/eaten/played it?
- Do I need this?

Going Green (a real-life story)

Rather than heading to the local mall in 2005, Wendy Tremayne decided to trade consumerism for creativity and organize a clothing swap. Inspired by Gandhi, who said, "There is no beauty in the finest cloth if it makes hunger and unhappiness," she hoped that she and her friends would be able to cut down on the nearly 10 million tons of textile waste that, according to the EPA, went to U.S. landfills in 2003. Since then, her Swap-O-Rama-Rama concept has spawned similar events in cities around the world and created a kind of participatory shopping by having sewers and sewing machines on-site to help swappers redesign some of their "new" clothes. It has also helped reinvigorate a kind of modern flea-market approach to shopping that is far more eco-friendly than regular runs to the mall. While Tremayne's events have focused on clothes, swap parties can trade any pre-loved product, from music to books to sports gear.

 iToast
www.myspace.com/toastysporks
15, Holy, Fiji

My high school had a student clothes swap. Buying clothes for the second time, or swapping them, reduces the amount of carbon emissions released into the air from transportation and manufacturing of the items. It really can make a difference.

Do This Right Now

Try these challenges to help you adopt greener shopping habits:

[green] Look at everything before you buy. Start becoming aware of packaging and recyclability.

[greener] Go a week without shopping (food not included). In your time off, identify something you need and find a green way to purchase it—after your week is over, of course.

[greenest] Research your favorite two stores. How green are they? Use what you learn to decide if you should stop shopping there. Or get involved and send them a letter saying you won't buy from them unless they get their environmental act together.

[super-greenest] Buy less stuff and cut your consumption.

8. The Community at Large

Spread the Word

Making eco-change beyond your immediate circle means engaging your communities. From the smallest (your family) to the largest (your country) to everywhere else in between, you can play an important part in spreading the word about the dangers of climate change and the real effect individuals and groups can make.

Face the Facts

One person's trash, CO_2 emissions, or water usage may seem like no big deal. After all, the environmental impact of throwing out a sheet of paper, not recycling two AA batteries, or driving a mile to the grocery store still might seem minor. But take a look around and see that everyone's doing it. Suddenly the potential harm mushrooms. Take the educational system as one small example.

- Although more than a third of all students lived within a mile of their school in 2005, less than half of them walked or biked to get there.

- Each school day, every student generates about a half a pound of waste. Most of that is paper.

- Each year, Americans throw away enough office and writing paper to build a wall 12-feet high that would stretch from New York to California.

What You Can Do

The things you can do to get your communities to go greener are nearly as diverse as your community itself.

Think global, act local. The idea of tackling climate change on a global scale may feel impossible. But if throwing away one piece of paper is part of the problem, then saving one piece of paper is part of the solution. Begin to change your community by connecting your small, local actions to their global implications. *micro*

Start at home. Start where you live literally—with your family—and figuratively—with those communities closest to you. You will have more influence on the groups you are a bigger part of. Then move on from your home to your block to your hood to your school to your town. *micro*

It's a small world after all. Getting one person to change may not seem like much in the face of all the pollution, waste, and emissions at the heart of climate change. But when it comes to climate change, we're all in this together and changing one person can have a multiplying effect as more people see that change can happen. *micro*

Sell our planet. Learn some basic facts and figures about climate change. Use them to inform and encourage members of your communities to go greener. (micro)

Know who's who. Advertisers spend a lot of time and energy targeting tastemakers—and so should you. Know who the decision-makers are at your school or in your town—keep in mind there may be more than one—and create a plan to approach, educate, and inspire them. (micro)

Always ask. Asking a simple question may be more effective than preaching at people. Does everyone come separately to your youth group meetings or your Saturday soccer game? Why shouldn't I print on both sides of my homework paper? Does the trash in the park get recycled—and should there be recycling bins? (micro)

Think global, act global. As you and your community make your actions more eco-friendly, each action will build on the one before it, expanding your focus from what can be done locally to what can be done on the global stage. (MACRO)

Larry
www.myspace.com/acalmlake
25, Green Bay, WI

Every sunday I go Geocaching/Hiking and I always take a garbage bag with me. Whereever I find myself hiking, I pick up trash to and from my destination. Every little bit helps...you'd be suprised.

Christina DGAF Crowe [imapowerrangerbitch]
www.myspace.com/104684312
17, Sunny San Diego, CA

Join an Ecology Club at your school! If you don't have one ask a teacher how to start one! You can organize fun beach clean ups or put up flyers reminding students to pick up trash or conserve water. You can even host a day where you invite classmates to plant a tree or water plants in areas of your neighborhood. You can decorate boxes to go in each classroom where students can put paper to recycle instead of putting it in the trash can, or paint trash cans outside blue or green so students can recycle bottles and cans. Good luck everyone! Work together to keep our hoem clean!

anne of the dead
www.myspace.com/wastedstardust
24, Nahant, MA

I've brought a bin into work for my co-workers and myself to put all the scrap paper we create and the drafts and documents that we do not end up using - we do a lot of extraneous printing and create a lot of scrap paper. I work in retail, and recycling is not provided by the company. As my town has a recycling program, I can collect this paper and submit it for recycling.

Okay, we've done the thing where we dissect your life and tell you all of the ways it can be made more eco-friendly. Now it's time to move on to the bigger things (but we still want to be friends, k?). All of the suggestions in the rest of this book can be applied to large communities. The strategy isn't so different, just the scale of your ambitions.

Family

Getting Mom and Dad to go green is challenging. It requires change, effort, sacrifice . . . and persistence. (We're thinking of how hard it is to get Dad to do, well, anything.) Let's face it: Many people—including your parents, perhaps—may not be interested in changing their habits. Just because you're related doesn't mean they're going to relate to your commitment to the environment. We didn't say this would be easy. And if we did, we were lying.

But never fear. Your enthusiasm may be contagious. Your efforts to change your family will depend on what your family thinks of your desire to get greener.

If your family:

Thinks it's just a phase you're going through like when you had an imaginary friend . . .

Stick with it. And remember that this type of reaction isn't logical, isn't necessarily about you, and doesn't have to limit your going green if you don't let it. Better yet, tally up how much less the family's energy bill is now that you're unplugging appliances and see what your family thinks of that.

Supports your efforts but is too busy to change . . .

You know that change takes effort. Keep up your own changes and they may start to learn by example. You can show them it takes less time and energy than they suspect to commit to a more eco-friendly lifestyle.

Is eager to learn more . . .

Duh. Help them learn more and come up with goals you can work for together. Check out the "Your Home, Your Planet" chapter for more on how you and your family can make your home greener both in- and outdoors. Then ask for more allowance. You've earned it.

The Community at Large

Your Hood

Figuring out how to green your neighborhood may seem harder than standing up for eco-friendly action at home. Identifying how the web of people, businesses, and city or county organizations active in your neighborhood work together (much less how *you* fit into the picture) is even harder. But because of the diversity of factions involved and the potential for change to ripple outward, neighborhood change can be truly rewarding.

- Go to neighborhood association meetings or events like local street fairs or holiday parades. Get to know who's active in community programs. In short, show up.
- Talk to everyone you can. Let them know about your interest in eco-friendly change.
  - Ask for advice—ask how their organization would proceed toward a goal.
  - Ask for advertisement—find out how they and their organization can help you spread the word.
  - Ask for action—get them to join you in going green. Getting a small, specific commitment may bear the most fruit.
- Find lectures in your area or suggest that your local library branch sponsor a lecture series on climate change.
- Join a community garden or consider starting one yourself.
- Plant a tree or plant where everyone in the neighborhood can enjoy it.
- Mount a carpooling campaign—starting with parents of schoolchildren and moving on to include others.

MySpace Action

It's gotta be said, and we'd be lame if we didn't say it. We love that you spend a lot of time online keeping up with your friends, but the computer servers that allow you to stay in such instantaneous touch account for an estimated 1.2 percent of the country's total energy. That's the same amount of energy used by all of the country's color television sets. To get more eco-friendly with your friends, here are a few steps you can take to be an eco-friendly MySpace user:

- **Eco-mmunicate.** Get in the habit of greener communication. For quick communication, use MySpace Mobile text messaging. A cell phone requires much less energy than a computer.
- **Make your status and mood green.** 'Nuff said. Use bulletins and your "mood" feature to broadcast your commitment to your virtual world.
- **Get a green screen.** Even though this doesn't *exactly* relate to MySpace, we thought we should tell you: If you're blogging or you have your own website, consider making your website more sustainable by using green hosting services. These alternatives power their servers through renewable energy sources, emitting less CO_2 than their mainstream counterparts.

Back to School

We talked about it at the top of the chapter, and now we're gonna dig a little deeper.

It's estimated that one in five people in this country spend their working day in a school—that's 55 million people. It may be the one community outside your home where you spend the most time. By working together with teachers, administration, parent groups, student organizations, and even the custodial staff, you can make your school far more eco-friendly than it is today.

- The assignment: Identify how your school's spaces and the habits of its students, faculty, and staff can be re-approached to make them greener.

- Ask questions. Start with your basic everyday school routine. Where do you spend most of your time? What do you do there?

- Do your homework. Evaluate what's already eco-friendly and what's not. Does the school recycle? Do lights and computers get turned off when they're not being used?

Paper Chase

Paper contributes to climate change not only by filling up our landfills with your bad paper airplanes. The number of trees that were cut down to make those neat white sheets and the greenhouse gases that were released by those trees also contribute to climate change.

For students . . .

- Buy recycled paper that's at least 30 percent post-consumer waste.
- Use both sides of each piece of paper either by writing in your notebook on both sides or printing out double-sided copies.

For the classroom . . .

- Each room should have a recycling bin for used paper. We recommend putting a basketball hoop above it.
- Encourage faculty to use the white board or overhead projector rather than handing out worksheets.

For the school . . .

- Investigate what kind of paper your school orders by checking the labels. Aim for recycled paper that has at least 30 percent post-consumer waste and is either PCF (processed chlorine free) or TCF (totally chlorine free).

[green] TCF (totally chlorine free)—Virgin paper that wasn't made with chlorine or chlorine-containing products.

[greenest] PCF (processed chlorine free)—Recycled paper that was made without being rebleached using chlorine or chlorine-containing products.

Getting There and Back

For students . . .

- If students in your homeroom live near you, arrange a carpool.
- Walk or ride your bike. It's a no-brainer, and it's good for you.
- Invest in bike racks. Aim for them to be in central, safe locations. Make sure there are signs pointing them out.
- Organize a "Ride Your Bike to School Day."

Myth: The school bus needs to be running to keep its engine running smoothly.

Truth: School buses today can be turned off—especially buses that run on natural gas.

Action: Investigate the school's policy on idling vehicles. Does your school allow it? Research the impact idling buses have on the environment and the local air quality. Calculate how much idling is happening. Present your findings to your principal and the other groups with authority in your school and ask for change. (Then ask for extra credit!)

Light Bright

America spends $6 billion on energy for its schools (roughly half of this bill is for lighting), and nearly $1.5 billion of this money is wasted. Nice going, American schools.

For students . . .

- When you're the last one to leave a room, flip the switch off.

For the classroom . . .

- When it's bright, use the sunlight to illuminate rooms and extinguish the overhead fluorescent lights. Recent studies suggest that test scores can be 15 to 26 percent higher in classrooms that use daylight.
- Put down the blinds when it's hot and the sunlight is strong. This will also keep cooling costs down.

For the school . . .

- Make it school policy that the lights should be turned off when no one is in a room.
- Make sure that blinds and shades function properly.

Electronic Education

Learning grows more high-tech every year. Our commitment to the environment should evolve with the technology.

For the classroom . . .

- Post reminders about the computer and electronics policy, telling students to turn off computers and other electronics like monitors and printers when they're not in use.

For the school . . .

- Make it a policy that computers and monitors should be shut down and turned off when they're not in use.
- Adopt the same policy for all classroom electronics, such as printers and overhead projectors. Do the same for other non-essential or emergency equipment in the school office.

Library (the room with all the books in it)

We love books. We love them so much we're in one right now! Here's how to treat our favorite part of the school in an eco-friendly manner.

For students . . .

- Create an inventory of books on the environment and climate change and give it to your librarian as a wish list.
- Check the library's recycling system. Are magazines and newspapers thrown away or recycled?

For the school . . .

- Include a reading list and information tip sheets for Earth Day celebrations at the school. Earth Day is April 22.

A school is like a complex organic organism: its different parts all have to be working together for a common goal to be achieved. You may have recycling bins and all the students and faculty could be using them. But unless the people who empty those bins are putting them into the recycling waste stream, your efforts and those of the community could be going to waste. Find ways to make everyone at school more eco-aware.

Get Active

Make friends. Influence people. What's stopping you? Your debilitating fear of public speaking? Oh, wait. That's us. . . .

Start an environmental club. Your efforts to make your school more eco-friendly will reach a larger portion of the school community if you can determine larger groups of like-minded people who share your interest in our planet.

Make it an assignment. Make your eco-interests part of your schoolwork. Turn a concern about the environment into a science project. Test the school's water. Audit the recycling practices. Just ask permission first, we beg you.

Reach out. Arrange for speakers to come to speak at school assemblies. Tap local green businesses to donate materials, time, or expertise for your school assembly.

Your Job

Be realistic in trying to get your after-school job to become more eco-friendly. You alone are not going to get McDonald's to go green. But you may be able to get your franchise to stop using Styrofoam or double-bagging. Start with small goals and make them work within the system. Areas to consider:

- Can the temperature be set lower or higher to make it more moderate—and less wasteful of energy?
- Could you and your co-workers carpool or bike to work instead of coming in separate cars?
- Could the amount of packaging or amenities (napkins, straws, ketchup) be cut down? Try asking customers how many they need.

Do This Right Now

[green] Have a conversation with a co-worker about your green ambitions.

[greener] Contact one community leader. Tell her about your interest in getting greener and ask her what your community is doing to be more environmentally friendly.

[greenest] Test water from your school, a public water fountain, or in a local pond, stream, or lake.

The Skinny: Green Blogging

Online communities can create stronger communities of friends. But they're more than just a way to keep in touch. They can also be effective channels to educate communities and to inspire change. Adopting an online theme—going green—can be a good way to show how simple steps to be more eco-friendly can be. Plus, when everyone on your friends list sees what you're up to, they're more likely to join in. So log in and start typing. Tell your friends about climate change and the things you're doing—that they can do, too—to be more eco-friendly.

emma

www.myspace.com/boatingismything

86, The Boro of Swans, Wakeboard Land Tokelau

My church is cleaning up the trash that leads into the white oak river. the river flows into the intracoastal waterway. all the trash has depleted the oysters which filter the water and now it is a unsafe area to swim in. it used to be a great place and we are workin to make it that way again.

Shelby
www.myspace.com/lovepeaceshelby
15, Long Beach, CA

i am a high school student and i have started many pro-green and economic awareness clubs at my school. i now have a recycling program in the works, all you have to do is learn the ins and outs of your school and write letters to the pricipals if necessary explaining how the school could go green, so many people are looking to help the enviornment but just dont know where to start- you could be that push in the right direction

The Big Question: Can you be an activist at work?

Advocating for eco-friendly change can be a second career if you're Al Gore. But you don't have to lose your first job over it.

Myth: Pushing eco-friendly ideas at work will only get you canned.

Truth: In the right environment (pun!), your efforts may be seen as ambition or concern for the company. How you present your suggestions will affect how they're interpreted. In short, don't be a jerk about it. Don't criticize. Show what's in it for the company, not just our planet, by suggesting how eco-friendly change can save your company money. Back those suggestions up with figures.

MySpace Action

Information travels fast. Share the things you're learning about eco-living with your MySpace friends so that it can influence communities beyond your own. Start posting a weekly or monthly MySpace bulletin about environmental topics.

9. Eco-activism

What Do We Want? CHANGE! When Do We Want It? NOW!

If you're reading this book, chances are you believe you have the right to a world free from pollution, and you believe you have the power to get government at all levels to adopt more eco-friendly policies. Or, you got this book as a gift, and there was nothing else to read in the bathroom. (We hope it was the first option.)

Climate change is a global phenomenon, which means it requires a global solution. While the individual actions you take to make your home or your room more eco-friendly do add up, there's a big difference between them and the broader actions needed to stop climate change globally. Knowing your eco-rights can help you get the government to act on local, national, and global levels—and it's the key to connecting your personal choices with the macro actions our planet needs.

Stand up for your rights—and get government to start standing up to its responsibilities toward its citizens.

Face the Facts

Concerns about climate change, global warming, and our planet have reached such a fever pitch lately that caring about the environment might seem like a fad—if the reality weren't so dire. Unfortunately, the gulf between the growing popular concern and the sense of a concerted government response is downright humongous.

- 175 countries have ratified the Kyoto Protocol, which commits countries to reduce their greenhouse gas emissions or use carbon trading to cover their increases. The United States has not.

- Polls conducted in early 2007 showed that 7 out of 10 Americans think the government should do more to try to deal with global warming.

- Among all states in the United States in 2004, Texas was the number-one global-warming polluter—and seventh in the world, emitting slightly more CO_2 than Canada. Everything may be bigger in Texas, but it shouldn't be.

Eco-activism

What You Can Do

There are a number of ways you can get the government to act on local, national, and global levels to be more eco-friendly if you:

Study eco-history. Find out where we've been and what we've already done for the environment. To learn more about the different government agencies and federal laws that are the infrastructure of America's environmental policy, visit www.epa.gov. *micro*

Track legislation. Knowing what laws—those that are eco-friendly and those that are not—are being written, debated, and voted on gives you the chance to have your say. To find out what your government is saying and doing about the environment and climate change, go to http://vote-smart.org. *micro*

Know your rep. Do you know who is speaking for you? Do you know what they're saying? Find out! www.lcv.org/scorecard *micro*

Vote. You may or may not be able to cast a vote. If you can, VOTE! (For clarity's sake, we'd just like to reiterate: VOTE, VOTE, VOTE.) Evaluate a candidate's positions on and fluency about climate change and government action. If you can't vote, you can still volunteer for the candidate you support. *micro*

Read or listen to environmental news. Your efforts to be more eco-friendly and get the government to go along will be more effective if you stay informed. *micro*

Use the power of the purse. Stopping climate change is only going to work if we find a way to both mandate and innovate our way to more eco-friendly lives. That means getting both government and business to work together. Use your purchasing power to effect change. *micro*

Become an eco-activist beyond borders. The environment knows no boundaries. Neither should you. Environmental policy in Beijing can affect lives in Boise. Learn about global initiatives that affect our planet and reapply these tips with a global focus. *micro*

Get active. It's our planet. Climate change is happening now. Stand up for your future. Sign a petition, write a letter, stop traffic and march—just not at the same time, because you might sprain something. *MACRO*

Take Action

Political action involves a complex mix of interest, rhetoric (that means public speaking), passion, communication, and connection. To push for eco-friendly action by government:

Connect. You are not alone. Groups of people your age are working together to stop climate change and to rally their communities and governments around eco-friendly policies. Connecting with these groups is easier than you might think.

Find them online. There are people all over the world working to make it more eco-friendly. You can find many of them online.

- Visit MySpace's Impact Channel to find out about candidates in current elections: http://impact.myspace.com
- Also, sites like Change.org or Meetup.com allow you to search for groups that share your eco-interests.

Look for opportunities to learn more. Some organizations and non-profits offer some nifty educational opportunities. For example, the League of Conservation Voters (www.lcv.org) teaches students how to get involved in election campaigns through its education fund.

Read an eco-blog. There's a lot to keep track of in the world of environmental action. You can read some of the more prominent sites. Set up a news alert. Use RSS feeds to keep on top of your favorite eco-blogs, or check the feed on our site.

Be a bridge. Environmentalism first became a movement in the 1970s and many activists from that generation are still around. Connect with them. They will teach you and you will teach them. But when they nod off in the middle of telling the same story for the third time, make a run for it.

Communicate. One of the most important things you can do is share your passion for the environment.

Speak out. Tell others about climate change and how changing your daily routine in small ways can have big consequences.

Write a letter to the editor. Newspapers are still excellent ways to reach people in your immediate communities. Your letter may also help drive the news cycle when newspaper editors and reporters see there's community interest in environmental topics.

Write a letter to your representative. If they're speaking for you, shouldn't they know what to say? You can find your congressperson's name and address at www.house.gov/writerep/.

Act out. You've probably been told your entire life that actions speak louder than words. In the case of eco-oriented action, it takes both. Target some important action to demonstrate your commitment to climate change. Green your public spaces. Plant a tree, vegetable garden, or a flowerbed. Clean up a run-down site. Pick up litter.

Demonstrate. Go to a peaceful demonstration or rally for the environment. Add your voice to the crowd's. Nothing speaks louder than taking to the streets.

Coordinate. Join national campaigns for the environment. Some to consider are:
- Natural Resources Defense Council's Earth Action Center (www.nrdc.org/action/default.asp)
- Campus Climate Change (http://climatechange.org)
- Friends of the Earth (www.foe.org)

Eco-activism

Organize your community to get involved. Different student action groups have guides for how to run eco-awareness campaigns at school. Check out Sierra Student Coalition (www.ssc.org) and Student Environmental Action Coalition (www.seac.org). Then tailor these guides for your own community.

Your Vote—Suffrage-ing Through It

Make your right to vote more eco-friendly:

Campaign. You can volunteer for the campaign of a candidate you support. You can also volunteer for environmentally focused non-profits that are playing active roles in supporting campaigns and educating the public.

Write to candidates. Get on their radar early with environmental concerns. Make sure global warming and environmental policy are factors in pre-election debates.

Check the records. As the environment becomes a bigger area of concern, it will be raised in campaigning. Much of a candidate's record and views on the environment will be gathered and made public by various reputable environmental organizations, think tanks, and non-profits that track this kind of information.

Share what you know. Encourage others to vote and make sure they're aware of each candidate's environmental position.

In the voting booth

Make the most of the moment (and no, we don't mean making out in the voting booth):

Primary care. In many local elections the deciding election is not the general election, but the primary. Learn the rules and register in such a way that you will be able to participate in primaries.

Study the dull stuff. Whenever the public votes on the real nitty-gritty of eco-friendly policies it's often through complicated referendums. Make sure you're well informed on what the issues are and what the text of the referendum says and means.

Think hard. Don't follow the herd. When you vote, make sure you cast your ballot with the person who actually represents your point of view—not just the most "electable" candidate.

Don't settle. If no one represents you, think about running for office yourself.

Eco-activism

The Big Question:
What can you really do?

Going up against the global climate crisis can feel overwhelming (after all, it's global, and it's a crisis). But don't feel disempowered. You have more say on these issues than you think you do.

Myth: If you don't have a vote, no one in government will listen to you.

Truth: Not all young people may be old enough to vote today, but one day they will. Elected officials at all levels of government know this and as a result are generally ambitious enough to give you their ear. After all, you'll be electing them to work for *you.*

Myth: You don't know enough to really change people's minds.

Truth: You *are* an expert. You've read 132 pages of a book about this very issue! And even if you feel less than informed, know that opposition to global warming is dwindling. Today, a majority of Americans believe the threat is real and want something done. The trouble is, they don't know what can be done or where to start. Your task is not to prove that climate change is happening or that it's dangerous, but to show others how they can do their part to stop it.

Our Town

Although the federal government has been slow to respond to growing evidence and mounting concern, local and state governments are providing significant leadership. Whether you live in a metropolis, a one-horse town, a sprawling suburb, or a subterranean lair inhabited by mole people, your town (or lair) can join the shift toward more eco-friendly policies:

Get a greener fleet. Government agencies have cars and trucks that are used on official business. Your town can make a commitment to the environment by choosing hybrids or vehicles that run on natural gas.

Rack 'em up. Encourage biking by installing racks in heavily trafficked locations where bikes can easily be locked up: on main streets, in community parks, outside libraries.

Get on the map. Cities around the country are joining green networks, from Cool Cities to the U.S. Mayors Climate Protection Agreement. Get your city signed up and start spreading the word. To see how you can get your city involved, go to www.coolcities.us.

Renewable energy. Cities can encourage less pollution and foster eco-awareness in their citizens by targeting renewable energy initiatives. It can have an impact: If just 10 percent of New Yorkers purchased green power it would prevent nearly 3 billion lbs. of CO_2 from entering the atmosphere each year.

Initiatives you can campaign for:

"Recycling on-the-go" program. Recycling shouldn't just be a curbside habit. Installing recycling bins for newspapers, magazines, glass, plastic, and aluminum containers on main streets and at community parks will give people opportunities to recycle and encourage the habit. It will also cut down on public waste. If it's good enough to do at home, it's good enough to do in public. (Note: We are not sayng that *everything* you do at home is good to do in public.)

More options for public transportation. Increasing the number of routes available on public transportation means more people can be served. To find more information on public transportation initiatives in your area go to www.cfte.org/success/elections.asp.

Bike rental program. Bicycle rental and bike-share programs are available in Europe and there are some early efforts in American cities to develop the two-wheel twin to Zipcar.

Stand on a centrally located block or intersection. What can you tell about your town's environmental priorities?

- Does it have public transportation? If so, what kind and how is the system powered?
- Does it have bike lanes and bike racks to encourage biking?
- Are there sidewalks where people can walk? If so, how many people do—and how many zoom around in their cars?
- Does the community have access to parks and gardens? What shape are they in?

The Skinny: U.S. Mayors Climate Protection Agreement

Leadership doesn't always start at the top, and grassroots don't always refer to people who have little or no authority. Although the U.S. federal government has failed to ratify the Kyoto Protocol, local governments have come together to pledge to reduce global warming emissions in their cities. Led by Seattle's Mayor Greg Nickels, more than 620 mayors representing nearly 54 million Americans have signed the Climate Protection Agreement and agreed to:

- Strive to meet or beat the Kyoto Protocol targets in their own communities
- Push for Congress to adopt greenhouse gas reduction legislation and establish a national emission trading system.

Has your mayor signed up for the Climate Protection Agreement? Find out at http://usmayors.org.

Major Eco-friendly Milestones in Federal Law

You should know some of the important laws that already exist—they can give you inspiration and show you where we still need to push.

- The Clean Air Act (CAA) was first passed in 1970 and updated in 1990. On average, you breathe more than 3,000 gallons of air each day, whether it's clean or not. The CAA tries to make it as clean as it can be.

- The Clean Water Act (CWA) was first enacted in 1948 and totally revised in 1972. It's been updated many times since then. It's the main law that governs pollution in lakes, rivers, streams, and bays.

- The Endangered Species Act (ESA) was first enacted in 1973. The ESA protects birds, insects, fish, reptiles, mammals, crustaceans, flowers, grasses, and trees from extinction. There are more than 600 endangered species and nearly 200 threatened species. The bald eagle and the grizzly bear have successfully been saved.

- The National Environmental Policy Act (NEPA) was first enacted in 1970. The NEPA requires federal projects to consider their environmental impact, and produce an environmental impact statement.

- Comprehensive Environmental Response, Compensation, and Liability Act (CERCLA or Superfund) was first enacted in 1980. The Superfund law was enacted after the Love Canal toxic waste disaster in Niagara Falls, New York. It imposed a tax on the chemical and petroleum industries and gave the federal government the ability to respond to the release of hazardous substances that can endanger public health or the environment. The money collected is put in a trust fund to clean up the more than 1,200 sites identified as Superfund sites.

- The Safe Drinking Water Act (SDWA) was first enacted in 1974. Whether you drink water from a tap or a bottle, the SDWA is the law that makes it safe for you to sip.

Although federal policies have left many eco-oriented citizens shaking their heads, local and state actions are providing some government response and environmental protection.

- In 2005, the Regional Greenhouse Gas Initiative, a cooperative effort by nine northeast and mid-Atlantic states, issued a proposal to implement a regional cap-and-trade program that will reduce carbon dioxide emissions from regional power plants.

- In 2006, California became the first state to enact a statewide cap on global warming pollution. The Global Warming Solutions Act will reduce California's annual global warming emissions by 25 percent by 2020.

- In 2007, San Francisco joined international cities in South Africa, Taiwan, Bangladesh, and France in banning non-recyclable plastic bags from major supermarkets and drugstores.

Eco-activism

Your Dollar

Though we hate to admit it, sometimes your almighty vote is not quite as powerful as the almighty dollar. In a capitalist society (that's us!), government influences and is influenced by the corporate world. Where the market goes, so goes government. Where government goes, so goes the market.

The silver lining is that you can use the power of your pocket(book) no matter what age you are (or whether you own a pocketbook). So, in a way, every time you buy something, you're voting with your dollars. If a million people decided to go buy a solar cell, it would be reasonable to conclude they're interested in solar power. And when a million people are willing to buy something, it's also reasonable to conclude the market will organize to sell it to them. So use your dollar—and get corporate America working with American government on going greener:

Invest in green. Whenever you have a choice between a product that's sustainable and one that's not, choose the eco-friendly option. If it's more expensive, consider it an investment.

Give 'em props. If you know a company is making real, sustainable efforts to go greener, you can buy from them *and* encourage them. Write a letter or send an email to say you support their efforts.

Use the suggestion box. If you're really in love with a company, but they're not selling a green option, ask them to.

Fortunately, American businesses are starting to wake up to how climate change is affecting not only public perception but also their future business. Several companies, including General Electric, DuPont, Alcoa, and Ford Motor Company have joined non-profits like The Nature Conservancy and Environmental Defense to create the U.S. Climate Action Partnership, which is pushing for a mandatory emission limit nationwide.

For more information on this initiative, visit www.us-cap.org.

Good News/Bad News: Green Business

Many businesses are suddenly seeing green—both in terms of the environment and the bottom line. From Apple's elimination of harmful CRT computer monitors to News Corporation's pledge to become carbon neutral, businesses have realized there's a large segment of people out there interested in sustainable products. Besides offering items manufactured through greener processes or return programs that prevent toxic parts from polluting our landfills, businesses are rebranding themselves as being eco-friendly and talking up their corporate social responsibility.

How it works: Trendsetting companies and consumers start paying attention to increasing eco-awareness. Consumers have more opportunities to buy greener products and services created under more sustainable circumstances. As they choose the greener product, the market grows and companies respond, making the market more eco-friendly.

The upside: Change is real. Companies are moving beyond their old opposition to being eco-friendly as they see how good it can be for their brand and their bottom line.

The downside: The number of labels with green connotations are growing without any oversight. Also, as companies tout their eco-friendly initiatives, it can be easier than ever before to say "at least they're doing something," without asking if it's enough.

Consider: Approach a suddenly green conglomerate with caution. (For more on greenwashing, see p. 103.) Do your homework on the depth of and commitment to their corporate social responsibility programs.

For more information on what companies are doing for the environment, visit www.csrwire.com and www.myspace.com/ourplanet.

Do This Right Now

Get a better understanding of what your rights are to an eco-friendly society. Learn what the government is or is not doing to give you that world.

[green] Read an environmental news site for a week.

[greener] Write a letter or email either to your local news outlet or to your representative and tell them why eco-action is important to you and what you want them to do about it.

[greenest] Join a group and go to their next event. Nothing will solidify your commitment to the cause and give you a stronger connection to the group like being there.

MySpace Action

Learn about organizations that are already making a difference. Where do you start? Check out the organizations that have friended the MySpace/OurPlanet page. Read about and add some of them as your own friends, but don't stop there. Investigate which are organizations that you can become involved with through volunteer work, donations, or other support, so that your online commitment is matched by involvement offline, too.

The Human Face of Climate Change

You don't have to be a wheatgrass-snorting shrub-kisser to want to do your part to stop climate change. You just need to care about our planet and its inhabitants. Good place to start: Humans.

It sometimes gets lost in the talk about the number of wildlife facing extinction, trees being clear-cut, and ice caps melting, but there is a very real human face to global warming. We see it every time someone with asthma struggles to get a deep breath. We see it in those places where food or water is scarce and people are starving. We can even see it where people are fleeing from war.

Why? The ability of different populations to maintain their livelihoods and their communities change as climates change. One consequence can be warfare. In fact, at least one cause of the crisis that has raged in Darfur since 2004 is the increasing lack of resources as the lands in western Sudan undergo desertification. And the oil fields of the Middle East intensify U.S. involvement in the politics of the region.

Of course, not every conflict has its roots in environmental changes and disputes. But many do and that number is expected to grow as climate change ravages land, water, and air thousands of miles away from us. So as you continue to fight climate change, consider how global warming and climate change are connected to human rights—yours and others' around the world.

The dangers of climate change are enormous and they are not going away. But don't despair. Look at the movement to stop climate change as an opportunity to prove what your generation can do. In doing so, you can become the new human face of climate change.

Start now in your daily life. You have no idea where it will take you.

The Janszenator
www.myspace.com/sensesfail133
16, I Play Scrabble in, Texas

One of the fundamental steps to living in a sustainable, more eco-friendly world is to raise awareness of the situation as much as possible. Once you've eduacted yourself on the crisis, tell as many people as you can and ask them to help in any way they know how.

ZOMBIEEE.
www.myspace.com/uncledjsrockettes
14, Dublin, Ireland

Even as kids, people should get involved in the fight against global warming, pollution, and wars. Eco-friendly teenagers just means an eco-friendly generation next.

Lorylicious![[♥rawr]]
www.myspace.com/pollita07
19, Chicago, IL

I REALLY HOPE PPL START TO TAKE ACTION ON ALL
THE DISASTERS WE ARE CAUSING. GLOBAL WARMING
IS GETTING BAD AND NO ONE REALIZES WE NEED
MOTIVATIONAL TEAMS TO GET EVERYONE INVOLVE I THINK
THERE SHOULD BE MORE RECYCLING, STOP THE WAR
BECAUSE WERE ONLY DESTROYING MORE OF OUR WORLD
AND LOOSING SOLDIERS THAT HAVE FAMILIES

Alexandra!
www.myspace.com/112103a
16, Phoenix, AZ

i think one way to help is get schools more involved with helping
out because the people we have on our high schools now are
the people that one day will lead this world. some how some
way we need to make people see that every little bit counts.
connect with people on a level they will understand. things they
love mostly.

My EcoPromise

As a citizen of the world and a friend of our planet, I embrace the fact that our planet is my responsibility.

- I believe that small actions can—and will—lead to significant change.

- I am conscious that all of my choices have a lasting impact on our Earth, and will strive to balance my actions to offset harm and contribute positively.

- I will continue learning about the environment and the needs of our planet so that I can effectively influence the eco-awareness of my friends, my family, and my communities.

- I will find ways to be involved in actively promoting change, and will give of my time and talents to join with others who are equally committed to our planet.

- I will continually challenge myself to find new ways to live a life that matches my ideals and my commitment to positive change.

- I will deliberately choose ecologically sensitive options over convenience in all areas of my life, and will encourage others to do so by my example.

- I will question assumptions.

- I will start today, with a single action:

Signed: _____Date: _____

Go to www.myspace.com/ourplanet to virtually sign this pledge and join with thousands of other friends of our planet.

Eco-speak: A Glossary

alternative spring break: Spring breaks organized around volunteering in ways that connect community service with education about specific social issues.

biodegradable: Material composed mostly of naturally occurring parts that can be broken down and absorbed into the ecosystem. Wood, for example, is biodegradable. Plastics, not so much.

cap-and-trade program: A marketplace system that creates a financial incentive to reduce emissions by giving pollution a cost. A cap is set and pollution under that is assigned a cost through a permit to pollute at a certain amount. Companies can then buy and sell these permits depending on what level of pollution is profitable for them.

carbon footprint: A way to measure the impact human activities have on the environment in terms of the amount of heat-trapping greenhouse gases that are produced. Expressed in units of carbon dioxide (CO_2).

closed loop recycling: Making an old product into the same thing again. Used aluminum cans are turned into new aluminum cans or old glass jars become new glass jars in this type of recycling.

corn-based PLA: PLA stands for polylactic acid, a polymer used in the production of everything from shampoo bottles to carpet tiles. PLA is usually derived from petroleum, but can be produced from cornstarch, which makes it biodegradable.

corporate social responsibility: A recognition of and formal support for sustainable and socially and environmentally aware business practices and policies.

electric car: A vehicle powered by electricity that is usually derived from batteries recharged from electrical outlets.

emissions: The gases and particles that are put into the air or emitted by various sources.

energy conservation: Any behavior that saves energy. Unplugging your computer leads to energy conservation.

energy efficiency: The use of non-traditional methods to conserve energy. CFLs are an energy efficient alternative to incandescent lights.

e-waste: The waste generated from consumer electronics such as computers, televisions, cell phones, DVRs, stereos, and video-game consoles. It's currently the fastest growing type of waste.

fair trade: "Fair trade" is an international-trading partnership that seeks equity between partners. It offers better trading conditions for marginalized—very poor—producers and workers. Using dangerous chemicals is discouraged by fair trade.

fossil fuels: Fuels such as oil, coal, and natural gas, which are formed from the fossilized remains of plants and animals in the Earth's crust.

global warming: The increase in the Earth's average surface temperature.

greenhouse gases: The gases—carbon dioxide, methane, nitrous oxide, chlorofluorocarbons, water vapor, and ozone—that exist in our planet's atmosphere and trap heat from the sun through the "greenhouse effect."

green hosts: Online hosting companies that power their servers with renewable energy.

hybrid: A vehicle that runs on an internal combustion engine that's powered by gasoline or ethanol and an electric motor powered by batteries. There are different types of hybrids, from the most fuel-efficient full hybrids like Toyota's Prius or Honda's Civic to mild hybrids to muscle hybrids, which use the energy gains to give the car more power.

Kyoto Protocol: An international agreement made under the United Nations Framework Convention on Climate Change. Countries that ratify the Protocol commit to reducing their emissions of greenhouse gases or to engaging in emissions trading if they maintain or increase their emissions.

LED lights: LED stands for light-emitting diodes, which are lights that typically emit a single wavelength of light when charged with electricity. They also use about 10 percent of the energy that conventional lights use.

life-cycle assessment: The methodology developed to assess a product's full environmental costs, from raw material to final disposal. A life-cycle assessment is used to calculate a carbon footprint.

LOHAS: An acronym for "lifestyle of health and sustainability," whose ethos is "responsible capitalism." A LOHAS person uses the power of the purse to make the world more eco-friendly.

LOVOS: An acronym for "lifestyle of voluntary simplicity" and in many ways is the opposite of LOHAS. This ethos does not support consumerism or materialism.

municipal solid waste (MSW): Garbage. It can be your old shoes, your gum wrappers, a plastic milk jug, or a cereal box.

natural: "Natural" food or products—with the exception of fresh meat and poultry—are not required to meet any government standards. "Natural" meat and poultry contain no artificial ingredients or added color, and are only minimally processed. Important: Natural, free-range, hormone-free ≠ organic.

non-toxic: Labeling something "non-toxic" seems to indicate that a product will not cause harmful health effects. However, there are no specific government standards for the non-toxic claim.

organic: "Organic" food has been produced using virtually no pesticides, antibiotics, or growth hormones. Look for the USDA "organic" seal. At least 95 percent of that product is organic.

PCF: The PCF (Processed Chlorine Free) label applies to recycled paper that was made without being re-bleached using chlorine or chlorine-containing products.

photovoltaic cells: A type of solar power technology that gathers energy from sunlight in solar cells and converts it into electricity.

post-consumer recycled (PCR): A product made from materials that have been separated or diverted from the solid waste stream. These materials are often collected in recycling programs and include office paper, cardboard, aluminum cans, plastics, and metals.

Check the score: A product does not have to contain 100 percent recovered materials to be considered "recycled." But the higher the PCR percentage, the greater the amount of space saved in the landfill and the fewer virgin materials used to create it.

renewable energy: A type of energy resource that can keep producing energy indefinitely without being depleted. Two of the best-known types of renewable energy are wind and solar power.

renewable energy credit (REC): A tradable certificate of proof that one kilowatt-hour of electricity has been generated by a renewable-fueled source. RECs are also known as green tags or Tradable Renewable Certificates (TRCs).

standby mode: The low-power setting for your computer or electronic device when it's not on but not entirely off.

sustainability: The ability to provide for the needs of the world's current population without damaging the ability of future generations to provide for themselves.

TCF: The TCF (Totally Chlorine Free) label applies to paper made from trees without the use of chlorine or chlorine-containing products.

Resources

1. Our Planet

For an introduction to what you can do:

www.myspace.com/ourplanet—MySpace's OurPlanet page is a good resource and the homepage of this book!

www.liveearth.org—homepage of Live Earth, which has information on climate crisis solutions.

www.mtv.com/thinkmtv/environment—MTV's campaign for breaking our addiction to oil and overconsumption.

For more on the science and facts of climate change:

The Climate Group's climate change site
http://theclimategroup.org/index.php/about_climate_change/

U.S. Environmental Protection Agency's climate change site
www.epa.gov/climatechange/index.html

Intergovernmental Panel on Climate Change
www.ipcc.ch

NASA's Earth Observatory site on global warming
http://earthobservatory.nasa.gov/Library/GlobalWarmingUpdate/

Natural Resources Defense Council
www.nrdc.org/globalWarming/default.asp

Pew Center on Global Climate Change
www.pewclimate.org

Union of Concerned Scientists global warming site
www.ucsusa.org/global_warming

Sites that focus on eco-friendly living:

www.thedailygreen.com—The Daily Green, an online portal for green living

http://earth911.org/—Earth 911, an environmental resource

www.grist.org—Grist, a news site with environmental news and commentary

www.treehugger.com—Treehugger, a media outlet focused on making sustainability mainstream www.worldchanging.com—WorldChanging, a site that investigates how to change the world through the technology and ideas that already exist

Sites with more technical information:

http://earthtrends.wri.org—the Earth Trends database from the World Resources Institute offers comprehensive information on current environmental trends.

www.realclimate.org—RealClimate is a news commentary site written by working climate-change scientists.

2. Health and Body

U.S. Food and Drug Administration
www.cfsan.fda.gov/

To learn more about the ingredients in your products:

The Campaign for Safe Cosmetics
www.safecosmetics.org

The Center for Clean Products and Clean Technologies
http://eerc.ra.utk.edu/ccpct/links.html

The Consumers Union Guide to Environmental Labels
www.greenerchoices.org/eco-labels/eco-home.cfm

The Green Guide's "Dirty Dozen"
www.thegreenguide.com/doc/100/10uglies

Skin Deep, The Environmental Working Group's cosmetic safety database
www.cosmeticsdatabase.com

Toxics Search from www.greenerchoices.org
www.greenerchoices.org/toxics.cfm

Eco-friendly eating guides:

Monterey Bay Aquarium's seafood guide
www.mbayaq.org/cr/seafoodwatch.asp

The Green Guide's summary of food labels
www.thegreenguide.com/doc/116/nonfoodlabels-ssc

The Environmental Working Group's guide to food and pesticides
www.foodnews.org

To find local-food options:

100 Mile Diet
http://100milediet.org

LocalHarvest
www.localharvest.org

Locavores
www.locavores.com

U.S. Department of Agriculture's farmers market guide
www.ams.usda.gov/farmersmarkets

Food Routes
www.foodroutes.org

For more information on water:

www.epa.gov/safewater/dwinfo/index.html—the EPA's guide to local drinking water

www.bottledwater.org/public/faqs.htm—information on bottled water from the International Bottled Water Association (IBWA)

3. Your Home, Your Planet

100 Tips from Con Edison
www.coned.com/go_green/100tips.asp

For more on offsetting:

Carbon footprint calculators:

www.epa.gov/climatechange/emissions/ind_calculator.html—the EPA's Personal Emissions Calculator

www.greenerchoices.org/globalwarmingonroad.cfm?page%20Toolkit%20 Carbonfootprintcalculators—a list from the ConsumerReports Greener Choices

www.ecobusinesslinks.com/carbon_offset_wind_credits_carbon_reduction.htm—offers a list of offsetters and compares their services

How to compare carbon footprint calculators:

www.fundworksinvestments.com/fn_filelibrary/File/Carbon%20Offsetting%20-%20 FINAL%205107.pdf—a guide by F&C Investments on how to evaluate carbon offsetters www.cleanair-coolplanet.org/ConsumersGuidetoCarbonOffsets.pdf–New England's regional non-profit Clean Air-Cool Planet's "Consumer's Guide to Retail Carbon Offset Providers"

More information on green and renewable energy:

U.S. Department of Energy's Green Power Network
www.eere.energy.gov/greenpower/

Environmental Working Group's clean energy guide
www.ewg.org/node/8139

EPA's Green Power Locator
www.epa.gov/greenpower/locator

U.S. Public Interest Research Groups (PIRG)
www.uspirg.org

Recycling information:

http://earth911.org/recycling/–Earth911's "Find a Recycling Center" tool

www.epa.gov/garbage/reduce.htm–the EPA's guide on how to reduce, reuse, and recycle

www.eia.doe.gov/kids/energyfacts/saving/recycling/solidwaste/paperandglass.html–Energy Kid's Page guide to recycling from the Energy Information Administration

www.epa.gov/epaoswer/hazwaste/recycle/ecycling/donate.htm–the EPA's guide to recycling electronics

www.nrc-recycle.org–National Recycling Coalition

www.greendisk.com/–GreenDisk, a recycling company for computer waste, including CDs

www.cdrecyclingcenter.org–The Compact Disc Recycling Center of America

For more information on composting:

http://aggie-horticulture.tamu.edu/county/smith/tips/compost/worms.html

www.howtocompost.org

www.p2pays.org/compost/

Resources

4. Your Free Time

Music:

Reverb
www.reverbrock.org—keep informed about what bands are going green

Electronics:

http://efficientproducts.org—guide to evaluating the energy efficiency of your electronics

www.energystar.gov—the Energy Star site has information on buying different energy-efficient entertainment gadgets

www.epeat.net—Electronic Product Environmental Assessment Tool

www.extremetech.com/article2/0,1697,2097765,00.asp—guide for building a "green PC" yourself

www.rbrc.org/call2recycle—guide to recycling rechargeable batteries

Swapping or trading in entertainment:

Video-game console recycling:
http://cc.eztradein.com/cc/
www.sony.com/recycle

Video-game trading:
www.gamestop.com/gs/trade-ins/trade-ins.asp
http://cc.eztradein.com/cc/QuoteCalculator.cfm?level%1&value%176

For more information on greener sports:

Golfing: www.golfandenvironment.org
Skiing: www.nsaa.org/nsaa/environment/the_greenroom
Surfing: www.surfrider.org

Other entertainment resources:

Green Press Initiative
www.greenpressinitiative.org/index.htm—information on green initiatives in the book publishing industry

5. Social Life

For more information on greening your holidays:

www.epa.gov/epaoswer/osw/specials/funfacts/holidays.htm
www.audubon.org/bird/at_home/Holiday_Greening/index.html

For more information on holiday lighting ideas:

www.energyideas.org/about/default.cfm?o%h,as&c%z,87

To find out where to go in your neighborhood to recycle your holiday trees and trimmings:

www.earth911.org

For ideas on alternative, greener gifts:

www.alternativegifts.com
www.ecoist.com

For a list of eco-retailers that offset emissions:

www.carbonfund.org/site/more/media/261

Eco-tourism & eco-vacations:

www.charityguide.org/volunteer/vacation/topic/environmental-protection.htm
www.responsibletravel.com

Volunteering for the environment:

www.epa.gov/epaoswer/osw/docs/vol4chng.pdf
http://volunteer.unitedway.org
www.idealist.org/if/as/vol

Alternative spring breaks:

www.alternativebreaks.org
www.mtv.com/thinkmtv/asb/2007/index_doityourself.jhtml

6. On the Road

National Center for Safe Routes to School
www.saferoutesinfo.org—online resources to encourage and enable more children to safely walk and bike to school

For more information on biking:

Adventure Cycling Association
www.adventurecycling.com

America Bikes
www.americabikes.org

BicycleSafe.com
http://bicyclesafe.com/

Bicycle Transportation Institute
www.bicycledriving.com/

Bikes Belong Coalition
www.bikesbelong.org

International Bicycle Fund
www.ibike.org

For more information on carpooling:

www.carsharing.net
www.erideshare.com

For more information on greener driving:

Better World Club
www.betterworldclub.com

EPA's Green Vehicle Guide
www.epa.gov/greenvehicles/

Hybrid Center
www.hybridcenter.org

Pump 'em Up
www.pumpemup.org

World Carfree Network
www.worldcarfree.net/wcfd

Yahoo! Autos Green Center
http://autos.yahoo.com/green_center/

To find out your car's fuel efficiency/alternative fueling:

www.fueleconomy.gov/feg/findacar.htm
www.epa.gov/greenvehicles/
http://afdcmap2.nrel.gov/locator/
www.e85refueling.com

For more information on car-sharing and renting:

City Carshare (Bay Area) www.citycarshare.org
Evo Limo (Los Angeles) www.evolimo.com

EV Rental Cars (Phoenix, Arizona, and Los Angeles and San Francisco)
www.evrental.com
OZOcar (New York) www.ozocar.com

For more information on walking:

America Walks
http://americawalks.org/

For more information on public transportation:

American Public Transportation Association
www.apta.com

Center for Transportation Excellence
www.cfte.org/state/states.asp

Trip planning on public transportation:

www.publictransportation.org
www.google.com/transit
www.hopstop.com

7. Money—the Original "Green"

How to find eco-friendly products:

www.greenerchoices.org—Tips from Consumers Union, the publisher of *Consumer Reports*, on how to read labels, suggestions about products to buy, and guidance on how to avoid being "greenwashed" by environmentally friendly claims that don't hold up.

www.alonovo.com—an online marketplace that allows you to prioritize your eco-values and then suggests companies that match them

http://thegreenloop.com—Greenloop, a directory of green clothing stores/lines

www.onepercentfortheplanet.org—a list of companies that dedicate at least 1 percent of their sales to environmental causes

www.climatecounts.org—provides information on companies and how they rate on climate change

www.thegreenguide.com/issue.mhtml?i=SSG—printable pocket guides from The Green Guide to make you a smarter shopper

How to find eco-friendly companies:

Climate Counts: www.climatecounts.org/scorecard.php
Co-op America: www.responsibleshopper.com
Green 50, from Inc. magazine: www.inc.com/magazine/20061101/green50_intro.html

For more information on reducing, reusing, or recycling:

Reusing Styrofoam: www.epspackaging.org/info.html

Buying recycled paper products: www.nrdc.org/land/forests/gtissue.asp

8. The Community at Large

http://gristmill.grist.org/skeptics—a guide on how to talk to a climate-change skeptic

School:

Campus Climate Challenge
http://climatechallenge.org—a joint project of youth climate-change organizations from the United States and Canada that connects high school and college students who are organizing to win 100 percent Clean Energy policies at their schools

Children's Environmental Literacy Foundation
www.celfoundation.org—the organization's mission is to promote sustainability education from kindergarten through high schoool.

Go Green Initiative
http://gogreeninitiative.org/—a grassroots organization that seeks to foster a culture of environmental responsibility on school campuses across the nation

Green Squad
www.nrdc.org/greensquad—the Natural Resources Defense Council and the Healthy Schools Network's guide to greening your school

Make a Difference Campaign
www.epa.gov/epaoswer/education/mad.htm—the EPA's "Make a Difference" campaign for middle school students

One World Youth Project
www.oneworldyouthproject.org—a sister-school program for middle- and high school students, linking groups in the United States and Canada with groups from around the world through community service around United Nations Millennium Development Goals

www.eere.energy.gov/buildings/info/schools/—the U.S. Department of Energy's guide to building greener schools

City:

Cool Cities
http://coolcities.us/—the online organization for cities who have signed the U.S. Mayors' Climate Protection Agreement

ICLEI—Local Governments for Sustainability
www.iclei.org—an international association of local governments and national and

regional local government organizations that share a commitment to sustainable development

Websites with information to use in school projects focused on the environment:

www.atsdr.cdc.gov/child/ochwebpgforstudents.html—Agency for Toxic Substances and Disease Registry (ATSDR), which is an agency of the U.S. Department of Health and Human Services, links to pages that students can use to gather background information for projects

www.epa.gov/students/—the EPA's student information website

9. Eco-activism

Youth groups for environmental action:

Global Youth Action Network
www.youthlink.org/gyanv5/index.htm

It's Getting Hot in Here
http://itsgettinghotinhere.org—a community media project that features dispatches from the youth climate movement

Natural Resources Defense Council's Activist Network
www.nrdcaction.org/join.html

Sierra Student Coalition
www.ssc.org

Stopglobalwarming.org's Virtual March
www.stopglobalwarming.org

Student Environmental Action Coalition
www.seac.org

SustainUS, the U.S. Youth Network for Sustainable Development
www.sustainus.org

Teens for Planet Earth
http://teens4planetearth.com/teenshome—youth activist offshoot of the Wildlife Conservation Society

Youth Service America
http://ysa.org/—a resource center for youth service organizations

Change.org and Meetup.com—search for groups that share your eco-interests

To learn more about what the government is doing:

http://vote-smart.org/issue_keyvote.php?state_id=NA—track legislation www.congress.org/congressorg/dbq/officials—find your representative

www.lcv.org/scorecard—research their environmental record

http://unfccc.int/kyoto_protocol/items/2830.php—background on the Kyoto Protocol from the United Nations Framework Convention on Climate Change

www.epa.gov/epahome/laws.htm—the EPA's list of major environmental laws

To find out what's going on in your area:

www.eredux.com/states/—United States Carbon Footprint Tables show you how your state's carbon footprint compares to other states' carbon emissions.

http://zoomer.sierraclub.org/—use the Sierra Club's tool to find news about the environment in your neighborhood

For educational opportunities:

Audubon Expedition Institute at Lesley University
www.lesley.edu/gsass/audubon/index.html

The E.E. Just Environmental Leadership Institute
www.eejust.org/

League of Conservation Voters Education Fund
www.lcveducation.org

Think tanks:

Earth Policy Institute
www.earth-policy.org/index.htm

Pacific Institute
www.pacinst.org

Resources for the Future
www.rff.org

Worldwatch Institute
www.worldwatch.org

For more eco-speak definitions:

www.nrdc.org/reference/glossary/a.asp—Natural Resources Defense Council's glossary

Environmental organizations and non-profits:

Alliance to Save Energy
www.ase.org

Environmental Working Group
www.ewg.org

Global Green USA
www.globalgreen.org

Oceana
www.oceana.org

Voice Yourself
www.voiceyourself.com

Federal Environmental Agencies

- U.S. Department of the Interior www.doi.gov
  - National Park Service (NPS) www.nps.gov
  - U.S. Fish and Wildlife Service (USFWS) www.fws.gov
  - Bureau of Land Management (BLM) www.blm.gov

- U.S. Environmental Protection Agency (EPA) www.epa.gov

- U.S. Army Corps of Engineers (USACE) www.usace.army.mil

- U.S. Department of Agriculture (USDA) www.usda.gov

- National Oceanic and Atmospheric Administration (NOAA) www.noaa.gov

Resources

Thanks to the MySpace Community!

peacelyse (Elyse)
Om Pacific
Fallen Angel (Shannon)
Lyric
   Rianna (Rianna)
Moochie™ (Steve)
Laura (Go Vegan)
   lynn
Denise
∴._.· *~ÈrIKa~*·._..·: (Erika)
ali[iloveryan] (Ali)
Chely (Shelly)
koder (Dakota)
Big Ev (Emilio)
LiZzLe (Liz)
In thought (Bre)
Jackie
Heybrook Ridge (Tony Bentley)
Temporarily "deleted" (Leslie)
emstyle (Emily)
Bet You Never Thought (Seth)
Tarula In D.C (Erick)
Wesley
Olivia (The Inconvenient Truth) ^_^ (Virginia)
Mean Little Mama
tarynpaper (Taryn)
so1o (Beth)
[♥]-lizz-[♥] (Liz)
MARIA ISABEL
Jo
Youth Energy Initiative (Byron)
AlexAli
Nico (Nicole)
Miss Cupcake Face Is A Ticking Time Bomb
   (Jasmine)
Tai ^_^ (tahirah)
Mr. Town's End (Josh)
Wolfman's Brother (Bryan)
Mountains of the Moon Eco-Fashion Melissa
   (Melissa)
Milli O.
Bethany
I dont got time for anything (Christian)
♥Angela♥
Bela Ray
GRACIE-LA (Graciela)
aLexandra (Alexandra)
GNaRLYx (Arleen)
April
Kyle
where's waldo (Rudy)
Stefana (Stefana)
arianne
FASHIONISTA (Gina)

FLutEs R hOtT   (Manuel)
CHRISTIN3 ! (Christine)
Kimberly
ZOEE:)
Nicanor
Joan
Robynn
Organic Lawns for America
Shawna
Jen
MixedDude
IAMSM (Sharon)
Jenn Bunny..<3   (Jenna)
The Awareness Art Project
Are you smarter than a blue crab! (Nelson)
John
Actively puRsuing someThing else (Joshua)
Yvonne
[HATE IS A STRONG WORD BUT I
   REALY DONT LIKE U] (Ashley)
Oh! Carley™ (Carlene)
XA Photo
Dharma Initiative Tequila (Elliott)
Diana
Crazy Sue (Sue)
Rachael<Oh No, An Eskimo> (Rachael)
Pashyn
Stacey
R♥BERT
Shannon
Kristin
»®¥Å/V« (Ryan)
Shelby
Lucky Man (Jason)
Rehab (Rehan)
Scott (Stanley)
Jamie
Salvatore
Kayla
Joe
Do something everyday that can change the
   world.
Colleen
enough is enough, if you walk away ill walk
   away (Lydia)
Heather
Lyrically Able(theNewBreed)
Rose ♥
Katjaa
altered imagery (Karen)
Fight Global Warming (Jerucha)
frankiedukes
Karen
abiola, host of BET Js Best Short Films

Amber Vae (Amber)
Andrew
JACOBeatworld
Lorylicious![[♥rawr]]
.:.♥Ranla Kaydolph♥.:. (Kay)
AmSymbols (Debbie)
ms. Grammie (Sheila)
Katie.
LadyLove (Melanie Marie)
Tammi
Chris
Aaron
Miz Trendsetter (Shelly)
Joe (Joe Shapansky)
jovic
Janie
Klaudina
Mr. Nowhere (Ben)
[physco ana] (Anais)
Dasone's Mom (Brenda)
Tctopcat
Michael-Angelo
Kachina
Lord Of The Nite (Chris)
Bradley
Little Willow
Patti
Angela
brocco...brocco-lee is my name (Steven)
Marg n' Charge (Margaret)
Steve
kelly
Ma
alia the great (Alia)
Starla
[hey] it's aj™ (Amanda)
;]MICHAEL[; (Mike)
Berg [has the new Armor album holla] (Joey)
mezzo piano (Christine)
Peter Patrick & The Tones
Karla [ZAPOLdesigns]
A.N.S
water head
daren
Grog (Nate)
Sheri (Sherilyn)
H to the L (Heidi)
♥Secret Angel Raquel♥ (Raquel)
Amalia
Leinani
jazzzgrrrl (Kelly)
Jaime
ChristopherJenkinsHolmes
Alexandra!
Nadiza
Sara
Hug a tree 4 me (Delisa)

teresa
paxton
Melissa
♫ DRE ♫
lotusdream (Carol)
Gabriela
Beth
Ginger&curren
em-c
Mags (Margaret)
Kimmie! (Kim)
Project417 Outreach Space (Andy)
jeanette
Val (Valerie J)
Kimosabe
Jennifer
Dyani
Coty
Jillian
Jeanbean (Jean)
Hello Clarice… (Clare)
♥Julie♥
kaciaboo (Kacia)
Re-Ya* (re-ya)
M!KE
Ü !!!! 10.12.07!!!! Ü
Jon Dubs™
Dudley, sweet and tender hooligan (Dudley)
InsaneMan
I⊕lalavanya
Tree Huggers of America
Chris
Ruby Red (Ruby Red Music)
Tracy (Simone)
Amber
☆アミ☆JescaX3 (Jessica)
Rick
Sarah
Short Peanut
Eco-Sapien (Julio)
Stayin Strong For Better Days (Anthony)
tyler [E! true hollywood story]
Sena (Nicole)
JATY Music .com (John)
Arlana (Mandahlyn Arlana Kayla Mae Dawn
http://www.myspace.com/lady_majenta
nerdgirl (Lori)
NURSE LEAH (Leah)
NickyC (Nicholas)
Mary Jane RottenCrotch (Rebecca)
CLEAN COAST COLLECTIVE
GENIDISIS (Candice)
Wil-Ma
pemian (Pedro Pemian)
Danny
David
Yasmine

What Jen Wants...Jen Gets. (Jennifer)
Linda Stamberger
boredom ninja...lol (Jen)
TerracottaSales (Brian)
sarah
Elsa
uniquelycara (Cara)
Giselle
Meghan
heather™ (Heather)
You learn nothing by doing it right..duh
   (Schesly)
little e (Erin)
Michelle
Britt (Brittany)
Dawn
Emmylou
Tracy
LAYLA!
Clarissa
Leslie
Cynda
Shizayne (Shane)
Saraherin.   (Sarah)
Forever Rebel (Brie)
Angela
Jules
:[CoolCat♥DAB♥]: (Catie)
Christina
little pink boo[x]RELOADED[x] (Quinn)
Project: Empty Hanger
Ash~Ben (Benjamin)
jane doe (Andrea)
Jax (Jackie)
blackmon (April)
Roselle
Natalie!
Shelly
Global Warming Sux (Anna)
Karen
Amy Larissa
Kristi
Cate
Ellie [Yeaya]
the canadian (antonelle)
Reading is FUNdamental (Becka)
jenifer
Shelly
Virginia
Lindsay
Pomona Wraps
I Want a Life that is Mine (Ashley)
Jacquelynda
runs with scizors (Drake)
christina
annie korn (Annie)
Shananigus (Brian)

Kay
Sheena
Tony
jessica.calloway
DIXIE
MARIA ISABEL
Jason Wolcott Photography
nicole
Future Mrs. Pflepsen
Magnolia
Jessie [Live, Laugh, Love] (Jessie)
street carp
Erika [♥]   (Erika)
deejay
Brandon
Sarah
Sophie Spirit (Sophie)
Queen of HaleyLand & DeanWorld (Haley)
Markus
sadtree (Bobby)
Ben
T-Rex (Travis)
Mickie
beverly
Mandii
Come To Mama Vintage (Terri)
Merry Mary (Mary)
Birdbits
Stop Socialism! Stop Hillary! (Chris)
salina
William006007 (Michael)
Reine Alyssa (Jeunes Belle Jeune Fille)
niche (Nichole)
Jenny
pigpen
Stacy©
hazriq -31- kuriro @ seNsaTa ii (Kuriro)
Starving Artist (Jen)
Kyle O-Saurus
Super[Dan the]man [Entangling Alliances]
   (Dean)
ann/captain jak sparro (Ann)
Jacob Daniel
karrie
Wendy
Sarah
emily<3
Shinigami Ookami.™ (Stephanie)
Eric Evans
Mike [Loves His Lollipop] (Michael)
Gennipher (Jennifer)
[T-Rex] Lex (Alexa)
CHRIS & tina (christina)
Brett (property of michelle)
Sara [rip lbw]
Miceli<3
Andy